AF608097

ECCLESIASTICAL COMMUNITIES AND THEIR ABILITY TO INDUCE LEGAL CUSTOMS

THE CATHOLIC UNIVERSITY OF AMERICA

Canon Law Studies

No. 300

ECCLESIASTICAL COMMUNITIES AND THEIR ABILITY TO INDUCE LEGAL CUSTOMS

A HISTORICAL SYNOPSIS AND A COMMENTARY

by

REV. JOHN PATRICK COOK, A. B., S. T. B., J. C. L.

Priest of the Diocese of Hartford

A DISSERTATION

Submitted to the Faculty of the School of Canon Law of the Catholic University of America in Partial Fulfillment of the Requirements for the Degree of

DOCTOR OF CANON LAW

THE CATHOLIC UNIVERSITY OF AMERICA PRESS

WASHINGTON, D. C.

1950

Nihil obstat:

EDUARDUS G. ROELKER, S. T. D., J. C. D.,
Censor Deputatus.

Washingtonii, D. C., die 3 novembris 1949.

Imprimatur:

✠ HENRICUS J. O'BRIEN, D. D.,
Episcopus Hartfordiensis.

Hartfordiae, die 8 novembris 1949.

PRINTED IN THE UNITED STATES OF AMERICA
BY ST. ANTHONY GUILD PRESS, PATERSON, N. J.

IN MEMORIAM
CARISSIMAE MATRIS MEAE

TABLE OF CONTENTS

CHAPTER IV

CHAPTER V

CANONICAL COMMENTARY

PART II

THEORY ON THE COMMUNITY ABLE TO INDUCE LEGAL CUSTOMS

CHAPTER VI

CHAPTER VII

CHAPTER VIII

PART III

THE COMMUNITIES IN PARTICULAR ABLE TO INDUCE LEGAL CUSTOMS

CHAPTER IX

CHAPTER X

CHAPTER XI

CHAPTER XII

FOREWORD

Customary law, induced through the repeated acts of a people, is true law. It is altogether proper that particular communities in diverse localities should be accorded this capacity. All law must be reasonable, and it is quite possible that written law may not in every instance apply in reason to each of the communities for which it is established.

However, commentators have given but little space to the body of laws governing the inducing of legal customs. They have given even less space to each individual law. The writer, therefore, has undertaken to present as comprehensive a study as possible of canon 26, which treats of the community capable of inducing customary law.

The dissertation is divided into three parts. In the first part, a historical synopsis, the theory and the law touching upon the community capable of inducing customary law is traced from the era of Roman Law through the age of the Decretists and Decretalists to the post-Tridentine Doctors. It has been considered preferable to present the historical matter with a minimum of commentary, since canon 26 in the Code contains a new *legal* principle, influenced no doubt by pre-Code theory, but not dependent upon it. The second part of the dissertation consists of a discussion of the principles in accord with the Code by which one may determine the community which has the capacity for inducing legal customs. The third part is devoted to an application of these principles to particular communities. Many of the conclusions of the writer on the community capable of inducing customary law must be classified as opinion, subject to revocation by an official interpretation of canon 26.

The writer is sincerely happy to acknowledge the debt of gratitude which is owing to all those who have encouraged him and made possible this dissertation. Among these he wishes expressly to number the Most Reverend Henry J. O'Brien, D. D., Bishop of Hartford, for having commissioned him to pursue advanced studies in Canon Law; the Faculty of the School of Canon Law at The Catholic University of America for their invaluable guidance and assistance; and his fellow students whose fraternal and priestly inspiration has made the course of studies a singular blessing.

PART I

HISTORICAL SYNOPSIS

CHAPTER I

ROMAN LAW ON THE COMMUNITY CAPABLE OF INDUCING A LEGAL CUSTOM

The importance of Roman Law in the proper understanding of Canon Law is not open to any dispute. This is most evident in the command of Pope Pius X to the collaborators of the Code when he stated: "... Idem [consultor] latino sermone uteretur, eoque digno, quantum liceret, sacrarum maiestate legum, in iure romano tam expressa feliciter."[1] In respect to the title on Custom in the Code (Liber I, Titulus II) the importance of Roman Law is best proved from canon 29, "Consuetudo est optima legum interpres," which is taken word for word from the Digest of Justinian.[2]

ARTICLE 1. *The Rôle of the Judge*

The thesis on how a community under the Roman Law could induce a custom was stated differently from the doctrine now embodied in canon 26, which supposes the possibility of inducing a legal custom apart from any judicial sentence. But the Romans were pre-eminently practical, and to them all law and the force of law rested on the effect it would have before a judge. Hence Julian, who served under the Emperor Hadrian (117-138) and is to be reckoned among the most illustrious of the Roman jurists, stated:

> When there is a case to be decided, and there is no written law to govern it, then the judge must protect what has been induced

1. *Praefatio Codicis Iuris Canonici,* Pii X Pontificis Maximi iussu digestus, Benedicti Papae XV auctoritate promulgatus (Romae: Typis Polyglottis Vaticanis, 1917), ab Emo Petro Card. Gasparri aucta, p. XI.

2. *Corpus Iuris Civilis,* Vol. I, *Digesta,* quae recognovit Th. Mommsen, retractavit P. Krueger (ed. stereotypa 15., Bertolini, apud Weidmannos, 1928), D. (1, 3) 37.

> by manners and custom, and if this be lacking, then what is nearest that and consequent upon it. . . .[3]

About one hundred years later Ulpian, who was murdered in 228, stated: "When one seems to hold to the custom of the municipality or the province, he must find out if this custom has been established by a judgment *in contradicto*.[4] By this Ulpian meant that the custom was of much more worth if it had already been upheld by some judge before whom it had been impugned.

ARTICLE 2. *Unity in the Community Inducing the Custom*

A custom, to have legal value before a Roman judge, had to be thoroughly agreeable to some community and in use among them. This principle is expressed in various places in the Roman Law. There are a number of phrases which indicate that a custom received its legal force from the general consent of the community using it. For example, Julian stated:

> Inveterata consuetudo pro lege non immerito custoditur, et hoc est ius quod dicitur moribus constitutum. Nam cum ipsae leges nulla alia ex causa nos teneant, quam quod iudicio populi receptae sunt, merito et ea, quae sine ullo scripto populus probavit, tenebunt omnes: . . . Quare rectissime etiam illud receptum est, ut leges non solum suffragio legislatoris, sed etiam tacito consensu omnium per desuetudinem abrogentur.[5]

And Hermogenianus of the fourth century declared that customs arise "as it were, by the tacit agreement of the citizens,"[6] while Justinian (527-565) himself proclaimed that customs arise *consensu utentium*.[7]

It is rather evident upon reflection that it would be extremely difficult in every instance to establish a unanimous consent on the part of a community for a custom. Therefore the principles as enunciated in the

---

3. D. (1, 3) 32. (All translations are the writer's.)
4. D. (1, 3) 34.
5. D. (1, 3) 32.
6. D. (1, 3) 35.
7. *Corpus Iuris Civilis*, Vol. I, *Institutiones*, quas recognovit P. Krueger (ed. stereotypa 15., Bertolini, apud Weidmannos, 1928), Inst. (1, 2) 9.

title of the *Digest* called *De Diversis Regulis Iuris Antiqui* will be of value throughout this treatise, and so it may well be stated here. It reads: "Refertur ad universos, quod publice fit per maiorem partem."[8]

ARTICLE 3. *The Type of Community Capable of Inducing a Custom*

In treating of certain express customs the *Corpus Iuris Civilis* gives indirectly some information on the size of the community within which there may arise a custom which gains the force of law in that community. The words of Justinian cited above, that customs arise *consensu utentium,* may serve as an introduction in the study regarding the nature of the community which may induce a custom. The phrase, "users of the custom," was understood as referring to the whole Empire, to a province, to a city, and even to a region or a locale wherein a community dwelled as bound together by natural ties, such as the cultivating of a given stretch of fertile land, the operating of a common industry, or the prosecuting of some common commercial enterprise.

There were imperial laws which had their origin in custom, presumably a custom of the whole people. Evidence of this is found in the *Digest,* which recounts the law on the degrees of relationship within which marriage was prohibited: "Libertinus libertinam matrem aut sororem uxorem ducere non potest, quia hoc ius moribus, non legibus introductum est."[9]

There were likewise customs particular to provinces. They dealt with difficulties arising within the province. Ulpian told of a custom in Arabia, where the courts severely punished anyone who prevented another from cultivating a field by placing threat-inscribed stones about the field. Regarding the gravity of threat and the force of the constraint implied in such acts Ulpian remarked: "Sunt quaedam quae more provinciarum coercitionem solent admittere."[10]

---

8. D. (50, 17) 160.

9. D. (23, 2) 8. The term *mores* is used often in the *Corpus Iuris Civilis* as a synonym for the term *consuetudo.* Cf. A. Van Hove, *Commentarium Lovaniense in Codicem Iuris Canonici,* V. I, T. III, *De Consuetudine* (Mechliniae-Romae: H. Dessain, 1933), p. 19; also A. Cicognani, *Canon Law* (Authorized English by J. M. O'Hara and F. Brennan, 2. ed., Philadelphia: Dolphin Press, 1935; reprint, Westminster, Md.: Newman Book Shop, 1947), p. 639.

10. D. (47, 11) 9.

Still, custom could arise in even narrower confines, such as those of a city, or those of a community encircled by natural boundaries. In the *Codex* under the title *Quae sit longa consuetudo* there is an interesting instruction to the provincial *praesides.* The *praeses* was the chief magistrate of the province, and he held court (or *conventus*) periodically in the chief towns of his province. The instruction to him reads:

> Let the *praeses* of the province decide the case before him in line with the proof of what has repeatedly and frequently been observed in the town regarding the same type of controversy, for the preceding usage along with the reason which suggested it must be protected, and the *praeses* of the province will take care that nothing be done contrary to a long-standing usage.[11]

A more particular example of a local custom is cited in the *Digest* in a decree of the Emperors Antoninus and Verus (ca. 161). In dealing with commerce among wine merchants in their particular localities it stated:

> ... with what measures or prices businessmen should sell wine is within the power of the contractors, and no one is forced to sell if the price or the measure displease him, especially if nothing be done contrary to the custom of the region.[12]

ARTICLE 4. *A Summary and a Preview*

One may well summarize here what has been drawn from the Roman Law in illustration of the kind of community which under it could induce a legal custom. The consent of the people in committing itself to a given usage constituted a primary factor for the inducing of a legal custom, although the sentence of one or more judges in recognition of the usages as established in a community was of great importance. One more fact is of special importance: nowhere was a com-

---

11. *Corpus Iuris Civilis,* Vol. II, *Codex Iustinianus,* quem recognovit et retractavit Paulus Krueger (ed. stereotypa 10., Berolini, apud Weidmannos, 1929), C. (8, 52), 1.

12. D. (18, 1) 71.

munity considered as having induced a legal custom if the usage was not attended with a problem that called for a judicial sentence.

As this treatise develops it will become more and more clear that a custom to be valid had to qualify as a law. That is why under the Roman Law a recognized custom had to stand as the answer to a problem which had called for a judicial sentence. The Roman Law principle which compared custom and law was referred to again and again in the glosses and the commentaries on the *Corpus Iuris Canonici.* The text reads:

> Ex non scripto ius venit quod usus comprobavit; nam diuturni mores consensu utentium comprobati, legem imitantur.[13]

Another phrase which was to be quoted frequently in the Canon Law—but not always with complete clarity—was that which referred to the effective cogency and force of a custom when it had become established *in contradicto iudicio.*[14] This phrase waned in popularity only at the time of the Decretalists.[15]

Again, in defense of custom, but also in due restraint of it, the Roman Law principle as expressed in a Constantinian Constitution of 319 rings out progressively more clearly:

> Consuetudinis ususque longaevi non vilis auctoritas est, verum non usque adeo sui valitura momento, ut aut rationem vincat aut legem.[16]

---

13. Inst. (1, 2) 9.
14. Cf. *supra,* p. 2.
15. Cf. *infra,* pp. 38, 44-45.
16. C. (8, 52) 2; cf. also *infra,* pp. 14-16, for the influence of this principle in the *Decretals* of Gregory IX.

Chapter II

THE *DECREE OF GRATIAN* AND COMMENTARIES TO THE TIME OF GREGORY IX (1227-1241)

ARTICLE 1. *The* Decree of Gratian (*ca. 1140*)

Inasmuch as this dissertation reflects particularly a study of the principle in law which touches custom, and specifically that which relates to a community's capacity for the inducing of a legal custom, it seems warranted to begin a discussion of the Canon Law on the subject with Gratian's *Decree,* for he was the first to treat Church Law in a scientific manner. Whatever is of value before the time of Gratian is included in his treatise, and so it is at least implicitly considered here.

However, before all discussion of the types of communities in which according to the *Decree* of Gratian a usage could terminate in a legal custom, one must advert to Gratian's proper historical milieu if one is to gain a proper perspective of his contribution to this problem. Gratian compiled his *Decretum* about the year 1140.[1] His work was the first scientific approach to the Canon Law, i. e., the first work which attempted to systematize the law of the Church — to explain the philosophy underlying it, to outline its sources and agencies, to arrange its laws in orderly fashion, and to evaluate the worth of the laws then extant.

Until Gratian appeared, the law of the Church had been growing of its own force, abstracting from the inherent restrictions that any scientific treatise could have indicated for it, and it expanded, as it were, in virtue of an *esprit* which recognized no express rules for the testing of the worth of the law. Very naturally, then, when there did not obtain any universal ecclesiastical law as established and promulgated by the Pope, laws were supplied by means of the particular jurisdictions, for example, the provinces under metropolitans, the dioceses,

1. All quotations which in this work are borrowed from the *Decretum Gratiani* are taken from the *Corpus Iuris Canonici* (ed. Lipsien. 2, post Aemilii L. Richteri curas instruxit Aemilius Friedberg; 2 vols., Lipsiae: ex Officina Bernhardi Tauchnitz, 1879-1881. Editio anastatice repetita, Lipsiae: Tauchnitz, 1928), *Decretum Gratiani,* Vol. I.

or also the monastic groups. When even such particular laws were lacking, or when no universal law had been extended to the various provinces of the Church, or when it had not been sufficiently promulgated therein, then customs arose to supply for the absence of the law.

In this light it is very easy to understand that by the twelfth century custom had become an extremely common contributor to the Canon Law. Customs of every type had arisen: universal customs with their roots in apostolic tradition (e. g., c. 5, D. XI), and customs founded in the practice of the Church at Rome, and then received universally with the passage of time (e. g., c. 3, D. XI). There existed also particular customs: many of them regulated matters which had been left unconsidered by the extant law; some of them shaped a more explicit interpretation of the extant law; and still others held sway in opposition to the enacted law, usually because they antedated the written law and thus were never discontinued by the community which held on to the customary discipline (e. g., cc. 3, 10, 11, 13, D. XII).

Since, then, custom of every type was so widespread in the twelfth century, a rather cautious attitude toward custom was formed by Gratian in what might be expressed as the following thesis: Customs, both universal and particular, have legal worth in forming law, but particular customs must be examined for their worth in the light of the written law and in harmony with the principles of law.

This thesis can be supported by means of two arguments: first, through a discussion of certain Distinctions in the first part of the *Decretum*, viz., Distinctions I, XI and XII, where custom is expressly treated as an agency of law; and, secondly, through a review of various chapters in the *Decretum* wherein one or the other single custom is examined in its potential legal status.

In c. 5, D. I, Gratian incorporated a dictum of Isidore of Seville (560-636) in order to evince the validity of custom in the character of law:

> Consuetudo autem est *ius quoddam* moribus institutum, quod pro lege suscipitur, cum deficit lex.

In c. 1, D. XI, Gratian adapted his *Decree* in favor of universal customs, these being more evidently equal to law:

Usus auctoritati cedat; pravum usum lex et ratio vincat.

Rufinus (to be studied more fully in the next article) in commenting on this section added:

> Porro, cum consuetudo legi non obviat, inconcusse tenenda est, et maxime consuetudo Romanae ecclesiae.[2]

Then, in c. 8, D. XI, the statement of Saint Augustine (354-430) regarding the "*particularis instructio* (which Rufinus [+1190] paraphrased as *propria consuetudo*) uniuscuiusque ecclesiae pro locorum varietate" was accorded full honor and acceptance, so that in this eleventh distinction both universal and particular customs were recognized as having legal worth in Canon Law.

Next, in c. 3, D. XII, Gratian gave his support to the force of particular customs with this quotation:

> Scit Sancta Romana Ecclesia quod nihil obsunt saluti credentium diversae pro loco et tempore consuetudines, si illis canonica non obsistit auctoritas, pro qua eis obviare debeamus; unde nil iudicamus eis debere vel posse resisti.[3]

But the two *capita* which contribute most to the specific interest of this dissertation are cc. 10 and 11, D. XII, wherein Gratian included two passages treating the worth of particular customs; in c. 10, of customs arising in a whole province, as in Gaul or England; in c. 11, of customs prevailing in a particular *ecclesia* — in this case, in Milan.

C. 10, D. XII, reads:[4]

> Item Gregorius Augustino Angelorum Episcopo.
> Novit fraternitas tua Romanae ecclesiae consuetudinem, in qua se meminit nutritam. Sed mihi placet, ut sive in Romana, sive in Gallicorum, sive in qualibet ecclesia invenisti, quod plus omnipo-

---

2. *Die Summa Decretorum des Magister Rufinus* (ed. Heinrich Singer, Paderborn: Schöningh, 1902), ad c. 1, D. XI.

3. Cf. Jaffé, *Regesta Pontificum Romanorum ad condita Ecclesia ad annum post Christum natum MCXCVIII* (2. ed., correctam et auctam auspiciis Gulielmi Wattenbach, curaverunt F. Kaltenbrunner, P. Ewald, S. Loewenfeld, 2 vols. in 1, Lipsiae, 1885-1888), n. 4302 (hereafter cited as Jaffé).

4. Cf. Jaffé, n. 1837.

> tenti Deo possit placere, sollicite eligas, et in Anglorum ecclesia, quae adhuc in fide nova est, institutione praecipua, quae de multis ecclesiis colligere potueris, infundas. Non enim pro locis res, sed pro rebus loca amanda sunt. Ex singulis ergo quibusque ecclesiis quae pia, quae religiosa, quae recta sunt, elige, et haec quasi in fasciculum collecta apud Anglorum mentes in consuetudinem depone.

It is important to note in this passage that Pope Gregory the Great (590-604) instructed Augustine of England *to choose* (*sollicite eligas,* etc.) from among the prevailing customs those which he saw fit to retain. It becomes clear from this statement that the legislator (in this case Augustine, a bishop and legate of the Holy See) was the proper judge of the legal worth of a custom. Nothing was said in reference to the duration of time throughout which those customs may have flourished, nor of the specific type of community that was inducing them; it was simply stated that they be the customs of some *ecclesia* (at least a religious body) and that they be in accord with religion (*religiosa*) and with the principles of law (*recta*).

In c. 11, D. XII, Gratian quoted from another Augustine, who had been faced with the difficulty of reconciling contrary particular customs on the fast. It is particularly noteworthy again that Augustine sought out Ambrose (333-397), the Bishop of Milan (374-397) and therefore an ecclesiastical authority, for an answer to his dilemma. The passage follows:

> Mater, Mediolanum me secuta, invenit ecclesiam sabbato non ieiunantem; ceperat fluctuare quid ageret. Tunc ego consului de hac re beatissimae memoriae Ambrosium episcopum; at ille ait: cum Romam venio, sabbato ieiuno, cum Mediolani sum, non ieiuno. Sic et tu, ad quam forte ecclesiam veneris, eius morem serva, si cuiquam non vis esse scandalum, nec quemquam tibi. . . .

Gratian, however, felt compelled to add a word of caution to this sanction of particular customs, lest the matter become unwieldy. He added:

> Hoc autem de consuetudine illa intelligendum est, quae vel universalis ecclesiae usu, vel temporis prolixitate roboratur. Ceterum, si pro varietate temporum vel animorum variae consuetudines intro-

> ducantur, inventa opportunitate, resecandae sunt potius quam observandae.[5]

Single customs were treated by Gratian in various parts of the *Decretum.* A selection of these will lead to some corollaries to the first principle of Gratian in respect of the proper origin of customs, namely, that customs must always be in accord with the written law and must fulfill the requisites for any valid law.

The first corollary is that in certain matters wherein the written law prevails or a custom has been prohibited, no community is permitted to induce a custom. An example of this prohibition is found particularly in the refusal to let clerics in Sacred Orders marry.[6] Another example is found in c. 12, D. III, *de cons.*,[7] wherein Pope Gregory I, when speaking to the faithful in Rome, castigated those "persons of evil spirit" who were seeking to disseminate among the faithful the practice of refraining from work on Saturday, and from washing oneself on Sunday.

A second rather evident corollary is that certain particular customs could enjoy a full legal worth. This has already appeared from cc. 10 and 11, D. XII, as already quoted, but it was expressed again in c. 14, D. XXXI,[8] according to which contrary customs in the eastern and the western Church regulated marriage among the clergy. The rightful existence of a particular custom was likewise defended in c. 80, D. IV, *de cons.*:[9]

> De trina mersione baptismatis nihil respondere verius potest quam quod ipsi sensistis; quia in una fide nihil officit sanctae ecclesiae consuetudo diversa.

A third manifest corollary is that an individual was precluded from inducing custom. On the other hand, a number of individuals not forming a physical community, but sharing a common office — here that of metropolitan — could induce a valid custom. The example is

---

5. *Dictum* Gratiani post c. 11, Dist. XII.
6. Cf. c. 1, D. XXXII; cf. also Jaffé, n. 411.
7. Cf. Jaffé, n. 1867.
8. Cf. Jaffé, n. 701.
9. Cf. Jaffé, n. 1111.

found in c. 8, D. C.,[10] where the quotation is from Pope Gregory I in writing to John, the Bishop of Ravenna, and saying that this bishop might possibly defend himself in the wearing of the pallium outside of Mass on the grounds of a general custom or a privilege: "Quod si hoc non ostenditur, restat, postquam talia agere neque consuetudine generali neque privilegio vendicas, usurpasse te comprobes quod fecisti."

In summarizing Gratian's contribution to the problem here considered one may state that he recognized the validity of certain particular customs, but that he preferred to treat the question rather cautiously. With reference to the specific type of community which could induce a legal custom Gratian offered very little information, except negatively in that he required the custom to be thoroughly subservient to the written law and to the will of the legislator. The note regarding the need of a legislative power within the community, if the latter were to be accredited as capable of inducing a custom with the force of law, preoccupied jurists for many centuries after Gratian.

ARTICLE 2. *Rufinus* (+*1190*)

To throw further light on Gratian's contribution to the Canon Law regarding the community capable of inducing a custom, it will be useful to cite the commentator Rufinus, who wrote a *Summa* on the *Decretum Gratiani* around the years 1157 to 1159. Rufinus had himself been a *magister* at the School of Bologna, and died as the Archbishop of Sorrento (1180-1190).[11]

In commenting on the *Decretum* of Gratian, Rufinus outstripped the latter in his foreboding relative to the rampant growth of custom. When treating of c. 11, Dist. XII, he stated in accord with the doctrine of St. Augustine:

> . . . *retineamus* illa quae scripta non sunt, sed tradita *custodimus,* quae quidem toto orbe terrarum observantur.

10. Cf. Jaffé, n. 1260.

11. Cf. Van Hove, *Commentarium Luvaniese in Codicem Irus Canonici,* Vol. I, Tom. I, *Prolegomena* (2. ed., Mechliniae-Romae: H. Dessain, 1945), p. 434.

In these words, especially with the contrast in the verbal moods, he accorded to tradition a definitely more favorable position than to the "things unwritten." He even qualified the word *tradita* itself by further stating:

> Non sunt intelligenda tradita ex quibuslibet, sed solummodo ab ipsis apostolis vel plenariis. . . .[12]

Again, when speaking of the custom of fasting,[13] he stated that Pope Gregory the Great persuaded the Romans (*Romanis suadet hoc*) to fast on Saturday inasmuch as they already observed that custom. In palliation of Saint Augustine's earlier statement that this observance did not bind universally, Rufinus explained that Gregory addressed himself simply to the Romans, and that it was not his intention then to promulgate a universal law.

Nevertheless Rufinus did recognize the worth of particular customs whenever the law itself was deficient, or when it proved inapplicable. He stated, for instance: "Quaedam precariae locorum consuetudine adiuvantur, unde et locales sunt."[14] Yet in a sweeping statement he reduced Gratian's thought on custom to a point which lent to custom a merely suppletory rôle in law:

> Reducit se Gratianus ad id quod inceperat, per alias adhuc auctoritates ostendens consuetudinem esse tenendem quae non est naturali iuri et constitutioni contraria.[15]

ARTICLE 3. *The* Glossa Ordinaria (*1241-1263*)

The next source which with reference to the Canon Law on custom may be investigated is the *Glossa Ordinaria,* an invaluable commentary on the *Corpus Iuris Canonici.* It will be treated at this point after the *Decree* of Gratian and before the *Decretals of Gregory IX,* for its chief commentary was founded on Gratian's *Decree.* The edition here used is the Roman edition of the *Corpus Iuris Canonici,* which was issued *emendatum et observationibus illustratum una cum glossis* by

---

12. *Die Summa Decretorum des Magister Rufinus* (*loc. cit.*).
13. Ad c. 12, D. III, *de cons.*
14. Ad. c. 4, C. X, q. 2.
15. Ad c. 3, D. XII.

order of Pope Gregory XIII (Romae: In Aedibus Populi Romani, 1582).

The finest contribution which the *Glossa Ordinaria* made to the problem here studied was its insistence on nine conditions as essential prerequisites if a custom was to prevail as having the force of law (*ad ius praeiudicandum*).[16] Some of the conditions are of only secondary value or interest to this work. These may be enumerated as follows: 1) that the custom be induced with the sincere conviction that the acts as intended for the future could be undertaken rightfully; 2) that the custom be concerned with a matter which yielded to the effective force of legal prescription; 3) that the custom be attended with natural equity; and 4) that the custom be not induced through error.

Three conditions dealt with the time element necessary if a custom was to stand with the force of law. These served as a hinge in support of the reflections which speculated about the number of acts necessary within the community before the custom could be called general and constant. The three conditions were the following: 1) that the usage have continued for the length of time requisite for the operation of legal prescription; 2) that the continued usage be sustained in a judgment *in contradicto;* and 3) that it be of long-standing and of approved character. The difficulty was naturally that of determining how in a particular instance one could judge securely that the conditions had been met. A helpful item was the fact that in other sections of the *Glossa* there was outlined the number of acts requisite if a custom was to obtain the force of law. Under the heading, *Quot vices dicis inducere consuetudinem?*, a variety of answers pointed to the need of an act's repetition twice, three times, four times, ten times, or so often that the act's initial performance eluded all memory.[17]

It is evident upon reflection that the number of acts which sufficed for the inducing of a custom could vary from a very few, even two, to a great number. This variation depended upon the possible number of times that the acts could be brought into play for the shaping of whatever customary usage was in question. In the *Glossa* there is,

16. Ad c. 3, D. XII.

17. Ad c. 4, D. I, s. v. *mos est longa.*

however, a line which expressed quite succinctly the rather relative importance of the number of acts requisite for the inducing of a custom. It reads: "Solae vices non inducunt consuetudinem, quia non exemplis, sed legibus, iudicandum est."[18] Moreover, this passage recalls the cardinal principle that no matter by what community the usage may have been practiced, and no matter what may have been their unity of action, the content of the usage had to constitute fit matter for law if there was to result a custom which obtained with the force of law.

The last two conditions mentioned in the *Glossa* as necessary that a custom could obtain as law were: 1) that the custom be induced with the knowledge of the legislator (*principis*), and not merely as the result of tolerance; and 2) that the greater part of the people have followed the usage habitually, for just as a minority of the people furnished no warrant for a law, so likewise it could not serve for the inducing of a custom.

> . . . quod sit de scientia principis inducta, non tamen de tolerantia; . . . quod maior pars populi consueverit illa consuetudine uti, quia sicut minor pars populi non possit inducere legem, sic nec consuetudinem.[19]

The first of these conditions was reiterated in another statement made in a gloss on c. 11, X, *de consuetudine,* I, 4, s.v. *legitime sit praescripta.* It was there stated that a legal custom could be induced *sciente illo qui potest legem condere.* The phrases, *de scientia principis inducta* and *condere legem* recurred with great frequency in the discussions of this era which dealt with custom, in preference to the earlier phrase, *populus inducens legem,* which connoted that the people alone introduce legal customs apart from any sanction of a legislator. For that reason, their import merits further investigation. In a paper presented in 1934 on the occasion of the 700th anniversary of the publication of the *Decretals of Gregory IX,* G. C. Medici offered a keen analysis of the origin of these phrases.[20]

---

18. Ad c. 11, X, *de consuetudine,* I, 4, s. v. *legitime sit praescripta.*
19. Ad c. 7, D. VIII, s. v. *consuetudinem.*
20. "Presupposti Giustinanei d'Una Expressione Canonistica 'Communitas Legis Recipiendi Capax' " — *Acta Congressus Iuridice Internationalis* (5 vols., Romae: Apollinare, 1935-1937), IV, 121-133.

In citing first the gloss quoted above, namely, "sicut minor pars populi non possit inducere legem, sic nec consuetudinem," he saw in that phrase a dependence upon the dictum of Julian, "nam cum ipsae leges nulla alia ex causa nos teneant, quam quod iudicio populi receptae sunt, merito et ea, quae sine ullo scripto populus probavit, tenebunt omnes." This dependence of the glossator on the statement of Julian led him to inquire further into the theory of custom in the Roman Law. In the *Corpus Iuris Civilis* this theory (the practice was progressively less effective from the time of Augustus in 27 B. C.),[21] as proposed in the statement of Julian, implied that all laws and legal customs obtained their obliging force radically from the consent of the people. In the Roman Law theory, then, it was the people who received and approved the written law and also the unwritten law, that is, custom. Medici argued that the glossator to the *Decree* of Gratian used the phrase *inducere legem* in this Roman Law sense. He maintained that the only proper translation of the phrase as used in a treatise on custom was "to introduce a law," i. e., to bring a law into being through the repeated acts of the people. This translation fitted in nicely with the Roman Law theory, but it hardly was applicable to Canon Law, in which all force of law arises from the sanction of competent ecclesiastical superiors.

To prove this point Medici showed that in the well-known chapter of the *Decretals* of Gregory IX, *Cum tanto*,[22] wherein were outlined the conditions necessary for inducing legal customs, no mention was made of the consent of the people as a means for giving *legal* force to custom. This chapter was rather adapted from the Constantinian Constitution of 319, which emphasized the prior worth of the written law of competent superiors over the usages of the people.[23]

Medici further argued that both Gregory IX (1227-1241) and Saint Raymond of Pennafort (1175-1275), to whom the Supreme Pon-

---

21. Cf. Cicognani, *Canon Law*, pp. 640-641.

22. C. 11, X, *de consuetudine*, I, 4: "...nemo sanae mentis intelligit, naturali iuri...quacumque consuetudine...posse aliquatenus derogari. Licet etiam longaevae consuetudinis non sit vilis auctoritas, non tamen est usque adeo valitura, ut vel iuri positivo debeat praeiudicium generare, nisi fuerit rationabilis et legitime sit praescripta."

23. Cf. *supra*, p. 5.—C (8, 52) 2.

tiff entrusted the task of compiling the *Decretals,* were men who were learned in the Canon and the Roman Law alike. Therefore, while they must have been acquainted with the theory of Julian regarding the need of consent on the part of the people for inducing a legal custom, they were at the same time confronted with the fundamental principles of ecclesiastical authority — the legislative power of the hierarchy and the moral powerlessness of the faithful to act contrary to its will as expressed in law. Faced with these opposite principles, they had no choice but to abandon the doctrine of Julian and to adopt the concept of the Constantinian Constitution of 319, which was more in accord with the principles of the Church in that it enshrined the connotation that all legal force of custom derived from the consent of established authority.

When this official law of the Church was published, the phrases *de scientia principis inducta* and *sciente illo qui potest legem condere* became increasingly popular among the commentators. Medici mentioned the interesting fact that it was Sinibaldus Fliscus, the later Pope Innocent IV (1243-1254), who in his *Apparatus ad quinque Libros Gregorii IX* (ad c. 12, X, I, 2) was the first to use the phrase *condere legem* in place of *inducere legem,* thus emphasizing that the established authority in the Church had in all things to be respected. An unfortunate result of this emphasis on the proper legal sanction necessary for customary law was that the terminology of commentators for centuries was clouded by phrases connoting that *the people,* and not specifically the competent superiors in the Church, *make law,* and not simply induce usages which might obtain the force of law.

In the *Glossa* mention was also made of the various kinds of communities, or groups, which were capable of inducing a custom. In a number of places a general defense of the possible rise of particular customs was offered. Among these passages may be cited: "Unaquaeque provincia abundet in suo sensu."[24] And again: "Dicitur ergo in hoc capite quod bene possunt diversae consuetudines pro locis et temporibus observari, dummodo illis canonica auctoritas non obstaret."[25]

Besides this general defense with reference to the possible rise of particular customs, the *Glossa* in another place incorporated mention of

24. Ad c. 8, D. XI, s. v. *regitur.*
25. C. 3, D. XII, *ad casum.*

three kinds of territories wherein a particular custom might arise, these being either a particular region (*terra*), or a place where a contract was entered into, or a group of provinces among which the custom became mutually intercommunicated or interchanged. The further discussion of the *Glossa* at this point stresses the prior importance of the written law in relation to custom, and the priority of legal force on the side of a general custom in relation to a particular one:

> Sed ad quam consuetudinem dicis esse recurrendum? an ad consuetudinem terrae? an ad Romanam consuetudinem? an ad consuetudinem loci ubi contractum fuit? an ad consuetudinem vicinarum provinciarum?
>
> Ad hoc dico (apud Gratianum) quod iudex, maxime delegatus, primo secundum canones iudicabit; deficientibus canonibus iudicet secundum leges civiles; deficiente omni iure procedat ad generalem consuetudinem, vel etiam particularem cum defuerit generalis; deinde ad consuetudinem Romanam, et ultimo ad consuetudinem vicinarum provinciarum.[26]

26. Ad c. 5, D. I, s. v. *cum deficit lex.*

CHAPTER III

THE *DECRETALS OF GREGORY IX* (1234) AND THE COMMENTARIES ON THE *DECRETALS*

ARTICLE 1. *The* Decretals of Gregory IX (*1234*)

What has already been stated about the legislation on custom as contained in the Decretals of Gregory IX will serve as a sufficient introduction for the study which *ex professo* is to be made of the Decretals themselves. But one may with interest point also to the changed attitude that developed in the general theory and doctrine regarding custom during the hundred years that intervened between the appearance of Gratian's *Decree* (ca. 1140) and the promulgation of the Decretals of Gregory IX (1234).[1] Whereas in the *Decree* of Gratian practically all particular customs were treated at least with suspicion, and only universal customs, duly respected at Rome, and rather of the tradition of the Church, received unqualified favor, conversely in the Decretals of Gregory IX particular customs were authoritatively acknowledged as a respected agency of law.

Hostiensis (to be more fully studied in a later article) gave colorful expression to the rather amazing influence of particular custom upon the law when in a passage he explained that it remained for local custom to determine exactly from what praedial and personal revenues the *decima* could be demanded and in what amount. He cautioned his reader thus: "Ne mireris si consuetudo tantae auctoritatis sit." And then he gave examples of the influence wrought by particular custom. It was through such custom that clerics were bound to continence, that the number of immersions at baptism was regulated, and that the status of legitimacy or of illegitimacy became determinable.[2]

However, the Decretals did not determine the specific type of community capable of inducing a legal custom. In this matter the doctrine

1. *Corpus Iuris Canonici: Decretales D. Gregorii Papae IX*, Vol. II.

2. Cardinalis Hostiensis (Henricus de Segusio), *Summa Aurea* (Lugduni, 1568), Lib. III, tit. *de decimis, primitiis et oblationibus* (30), n. 16.

of the Decretals simply relied, so it seems, on the parallel that was acknowledged to exist between custom and law as juridical factors of similar import. It will be shown that two principles as deriving from this parallel were recurrently stressed in the Decretals. The first was the principle that no matter how extensive the community in which a usage had obtained, it could be impugned by a competent legislator. The second was the principle that the community which observed the usage had to be such that it was subject as a moral unit to the legislator who was empowered to honor the usage as a legal custom through his approval of it.

It has already been explained in accordance with a statement borrowed from Medici[3] that Raymond of Pennafort abandoned the theory of the Roman jurist Julian, which theory maintained that the people of the community itself radically gave their sanction to all their laws and legal customs. Instead, Raymond of Pennafort chose to incorporate in the Decretals the Constantinian Constitution of 319, which emphasized the principle that all legal force of custom derived from the consent of established authority.

The importance of the legislator was time and again stressed in Gregory IX's Decretals. A canon taken from the IV General Council of the Lateran (1215) reads:

> Ut autem correctionis et reformationis officium libere Episcopi valeant exercere, decernimus, ut exsecutionem ipsorum nulla consuetudo vel appellatio valeat impedire. . . .[4]

Though this canon of the Fourth Lateran Council vindicated for bishops a disciplinary rather than a legislative power, it plainly insinuated that customs were to be kept in check and restraint by the proper ecclesiastical authority.

Some years earlier Pope Lucius III (1181-1185) had written to the Archbishop of Gran (Esztergom, in Hungary) and with reference to the regulation of the payment of tithes had advised him thus:

---

3. Cf. *supra,* pp. 14-16.

4. C. 13, X, *de officio iudicis ordinarii,* I, 31. This decretal reproduced can. 7 of the Council.

> ... quoniam a diversis diversa consuetudo tenetur, *tu eligas* in hoc casu, quod per consuetudinem diu obtentam, ibidem noveris observatum.[5]

Another passage from this rescript is worth adding parenthetically, for in it the Supreme Pontiff makes humble confession of the complexity of custom, saying, " . . . licet immeriti, pro scientiae nostrae modo, respondere cogimur consultationem singulorum."[6]

In c. 3, X, *de consuetudine,* I, 4, the so-called custom in the diocese of Poitiers, namely, of passing sentence according to the prevailing opinion of all those present — the literate and the illiterate, the wise and the unwise — was prohibited. In this decretal power of determining the law, and, by implication, the capacity of establishing a custom which could obtain with the force of law, were removed from the people as a group.

> Ad nostram audientiam noveris pervenisse, quod in tua dioecesi etiam in causis ecclesiasticis consuetudo minus rationabilis habeatur, quod, cum aliqua causa tractatur ibidem . . . a praesentibus literatis et illiteratis, sapientibus et insipientibus, quid iuris sit quaeritur, et quod illi dictaverint vel aliquis eorum, praesentium consilio requisito pro sententia teneatur. Nos igitur attendentes, quod consuetudo, quae canonicis obviat institutis, nullius debeat esse momenti, cum sententia a non suo iudice lata nullam obtineat firmitatem, ut in causis ecclesiasticis subiectorum tuorum, postquam tibi de meritis earum constiterit, sententiam proferre valeas, sicut ordo postulat *rationis,* auctoritate tibi praesentium, praemissa consuetudine *non obstante,* concedimus facultatem.[7]

While it remained true that a legal custom could arise solely through the concerted acts of a group, yet in this instance a restraint was put upon the people against overriding the authority of the legally constituted judge.

---

5. C. 20, X, *de decimis, primitiis, et oblationibus,* III, 30 (italics added). Cf. Jaffé, n. 15196.

6. *Loc. cit.*

7. Cf. Potthast, *Regesta Pontificum Romanorum inde ab anno post Christum natum MCXCVIII ad annum MCCCIV* (2 vols., Berolini, 1874-1875), n. 604 (hereafter cited Potthast). The italics in the text are added by the writer.

The second principle highlighted in the Decretals of Gregory IX insisted that before a community could induce a custom it had to be such that it was subject as a moral unit to the legislator who through judicial or administrative competence was empowered to honor the usage as a legal custom through his approval of it.

A rather evident vindication for this principle seemed warranted *a priori.* The Decretals of Gregory IX treated exclusively of Church Law. Yet in the Decretals custom was given a prominent place as an agency of law.[8] Accordingly, as such an agency of law custom likewise was regulated by the principles of law.

A second vindication derived from the distinction that existed between custom and prescription. Though this distinction appeared only implicitly in the Decretals, it was brought into sharp relief by the commentators. Hostiensis[9] pointed out that custom was essentially the work of a community, and its end the acquisition of a right, while prescription was operable on the part of a single person, and simply excluded others from pressing a right which once they could have asserted:

> n. 6 . . . requiritur quod maior pars populi sic usa fuerit . . . quia unus solus non possit allegare consuetudinem.
>
> n. 12 . . . praescriptio acquiritur singulari et privato. Sed consuetudo non acquiritur magis isti quam illi.
>
> n. 14 . . . praescriptio de natura sua est actionis sive iuris petendi exclusio . . . sed consuetudo de natura sua est actionis sive iuris acquisitio.

A final vindication for this second principle may be derived through a cursory glance at various of the particular customs mentioned in Gregory IX's Decretals. If a critic should counter that this argument unwarrantedly generalizes from particulars, one could reply that the induction of some principle from the related uniform facts seems preferable indeed to leaving the facts stand as isolated events devoid of all juridical import.

The first example is taken from c. 2, X, *de consuetudine,* I, 4,[10] wherein the particular custom of *scotatio* received mention. By this

8. X, *de consuetudine,* I, 4.

9. *Summa Aurea,* Lib. I, tit. 4, nn. 6, 12, 14.

10. Cf. Potthast, n. 424.

custom a person could will a tract of land to the church simply by gathering a handful of earth from it and giving it to the bishop or to some other prelate to be placed on the altar in the presence of witnesses. This custom prevailed throughout the kingdom of Dacia, and Innocent III gave it his sanction in instructing the Archbishop of Lyons (a legislator like the Supreme Pontiff) to sustain it.

Another example is taken from c. 8, X, *de consuetudine,* I, 4, and concerned a particular custom which affected just two single monasteries. The *fratres Karofenses* alleged that there existed a custom (*approbata ab episcopo Moriensi*) whereby the abbot of the *fratres Andrenses* was to be selected from among the *Karofenses* at the choice of the *fratres Andrenses.* Pope Innocent III in 1209 settled the dispute with these words:

> . . . mandamus, quatenus . . . si ex parte Karofensis coenobii talis fuerit consuetudo probata, quae iuri communi praeiudicet, in hac parte vos secundum illam consuetudinem decernatis electionem Andrensis abbatis de cetero faciendam: alioquin, quodsi talis consuetudo probata non fuerit, per quam in hoc casu praeiudicetur iuri communi, vos Andrensibus monachis ius eligendi abbatem . . . adiudicare curetis. . . .

Of first importance in this decree was not the size or the nature of the community involved, but the legal *approval* which, as sustainable in a judicial sentence, had been attached to their custom.

A further study of the notion of an *approved* custom seems called for, since the mention of such an approved custom occurs so often in the Decretal Law. In his chapter on the Decretals of Gregory IX, Wehrlé added a lengthy footnote, wherein he listed the multiplied canons that employ the phrase *consuetudo approbata.*[11] He then inquired into the exact meaning of this phrase. Inherently one could of course espouse the opinion, so he stated, that it refers to an approval consequent on the lapse of time (*coutume approuvée par les actes, approbata actibus utentium*). But, so he continued, one could likewise with serious reason assert that it refers to an approval deriving from authority (*coutume approuvée par l'autorité*). This, he felt, appeared to be the natural

11. Wehrlé, *De la Coutume dans le Droit Canonique* (Paris: Librairie du Recueil Sirey, 1928), p. 134, footnote 1.

meaning of the phrase, and surely was warranted in certain more express chapters of the Decretals.

He concluded that the best solution of the difficulty rested in the assumption that the phrase did signify, up to the close of the twelfth century, an approval which simply involved the element of time; but that from the time of Innocent III onward the phrase connoted an approval deriving from authority. This approval was to be understood, not as granted arbitrarily, but as having previously reckoned with the duration, the reasonableness and the usefulness of the custom as warranting a favorable judgment regarding its legal worth. Wehrlé in the body of his text which gave rise to the footnote stated without qualification that a custom *once approved by the legislator* constituted a right as valuable as the written law.

This interpretation of an *approved custom,* as one sanctioned by competent ecclesiastical authority, is in full accord with the opinion of Medici.[12] It was he, one recalls, who stated that the theory of the Roman jurist Julian, who averred that it was the community which induced the custom that gave it legal worth, ceded with the advent of the Decretals of Gregory IX to the statement that only competent superiors could sanction law, whether written or customary.

In confirmation, then, of the prevailing requisite of an authoritative sanction if a commonly observed usage was to grow to the stature of a legal custom, one may effectively point to still another Gregorian decretal. It incorporated anew the Constantinian Constitution, to which Medici attached so much importance.[13]

The matter under dispute was the sale of a house to two laymen by the archpresbyter of the church of St. Anastasia in the city of Verona. The validity of the sale was contested by the other clerics of this church. These sustained a twofold adverse sentence in view of the custom then extant in the city of Verona. But Alexander III (1159-1181) reversed the decision with these words: "... licet usus vel consuetudinis non minima sit auctoritas, numquam tamen veritati aut legi praeiudicat."

12. Cf. *supra,* pp. 14-16.

13. C. 8, X, II, *de sententia et re iudicata,* 27; cf. Jaffé, n. 8183.

In a word, then, it may be said that while Gregory IX recognized the legal force of custom, both universal and particular, he made that legal status thoroughly dependent upon legislative authority, both in its initial sanction and in its continuing force.

ARTICLE 2. *The* Decretals of Boniface VIII (*1298*)

There is need here of referring to but a single decretal in the *Liber Sextus* of Boniface VIII.[14] This decretal was cited by the commentators quite consistently. It stated that the Supreme Pontiff is presumed to hold all laws *in scrinio pectoris sui.* When, therefore, he made a new law, it was to be understood that he revoked every prior contrary law even when he had left such a law unmentioned. But then the Pope continued:

> . . . quia tamen locorum specialium et personarum singularium consuetudines et statuta, quum sint facti et in facto consistant, potest probabiliter ignorare: ipsis, dum tamen sint rationabilia, per constitutionem a se noviter editam, nisi expresse caveatur in ipsa, non intelligitur in aliquo derogare.[15]

The importance of this statement can be best understood if one summarizes briefly what will be more fully developed in the next articles. The fact that an approved custom had the force of law was always recognized by canonical authors. This postulated the need of a sanction from one who possessed legislative power by means of which he could attach legal worth to the custom. But in this statement of Boniface VIII "customs of special places and of particular persons" were accorded the prerogative of continuing as binding law even in the face of any contrary universal law enacted by the Roman Pontiff, provided only that he did not advert to them expressly. Thus the retention of such customs, though contrary to the newly enacted pontifical law, was not in any way conditioned on any express pontifical approval of them.

---

14. *Corpus Iuris Canonici, Liber Sextus Decretalium D. Bonifacii Papae VIII,* Vol. II — c. 1, *de constitutionibus,* I, 2, in VI°.

15. *Loc. cit.*

ARTICLE 3. *Saint Thomas Aquinas (1225-1274)*

Saint Thomas Aquinas made a great contribution to the theory on custom in presenting an explanation of the relative parts played by the people and the legislator in the forming of a valid custom. He perceived that in a society the people might or might not be free to make laws for themselves. But he taught that in either society a custom could arise from the people and acquire legal force. He stated the case thus:

> ... multitudo in qua consuetudo introducitur duplicis conditionis esse potest. Si enim sit libera multitudo quae possit sibi legem facere, plus est consensus totius multitudinis ad aliquid observandum, quod consuetudo manifestat, quam auctoritas principis.... Si vero multitudo non habeat liberam potestatem condendi sibi legem, vel legem a superiore potestate positam removendi, tamen ipsa consuetudo in tali multitudine praevalens obtinet vim legis, inquantum per eos toleratur ad quos pertinet multitudini legem imponere; ex hoc enim ipso videntur approbare quod consuetudo introduxit.[16]

The second category, that in which the people constituting the society are not free to establish law for themselves, is the one in which the Church is included. The terms which St. Thomas used in his explanation were already in use among the commentators of Canon Law. The phrase *condere legem* had shortly before been brought into use by Sinibaldus Fliscus,[17] and it was thereafter to recur often. However, the phrase *per eos toleratur ad quos pertinet multitudini legem imponere* became somewhat qualified in the *Glossa Ordinaria,*[18] and it received further consideration from the later commentators. But the principle embodied in the teaching of Saint Thomas, namely, that the community induces the custom in its factual elements, but that the competent legislator accords to it the needed legal sanction, has endured to the present day.

---

16. Thomas Aquinas, *Summa Theologica* (ed. Marietti, 6 vols., Taurini Romae: Marietti, 1937), Ia IIae, q. 97, art. 3, *ad 3um.*

17. Cf. *supra,* p. 16.

18. Cf. *supra,* p. 14.

ARTICLE 4. *Hostiensis (+1271)*

A second commentator worthy of study in the question here discussed is Hostiensis (Henricus Cardinalis de Segusio), who died as Cardinal of Ostia in 1271. He wrote a *Summa Aurea,* particularly on the Decretals of Gregory IX, around the years 1250-1253.[19] The comment of Hostiensis on the "amazing" influence of custom in the formation of law has already been noted.[20]

In his *Summa* Hostiensis has a passage beginning, *Quatuor sunt species consuetudinis,* which is of particular interest in the present discussion.[21] He listed the species as four: very general, general, special or particular, and very particular. But it is what in the explanation of these species he contributed to the theory on the community capable of inducing a legal custom that is most profitable. For the crux of this problem is to determine with what minimum conditions and elements any existing community could qualify for the inducing of a custom that could obtain the force of law.

The very general species, with the example he chose that all Catholics customarily pray toward the East, was simply the universal custom which was never the subject of dispute.

The general custom was one whose formation derived from a community which represented an entire province. The example offered by Hostiensis was that of the custom whereby throughout the province of Tuscia the administration of prebends was the concern of the *capitulum* alone, and not also of the bishop ordinary. This example could be regarded as an excellent illustration of the impact of custom in particular territories on the common law of the Church.

The special or particular custom was the one which obtained exclusively in one city, or in some particular place (*in alio loco* — a locale, reminiscent of the Roman Law provision for communities surrounded by natural boundaries).[22] In this species Hostiensis left room for a distinction between two separate categories of persons who were members of that community. If an existing custom implied an obliga-

19. Cf. Van Hove, *Prolegomena,* p. 476.
20. Cf. *supra,* p. 18.
21. Cf. Hostiensis, *Summa Aurea,* Lib. I, tit. 4, *de consuetudine,* nn. 11-12.
22. Cf. *supra,* p. 3.

tion for the laity, then its observance did not weigh upon clerics, "nisi et inter ipsos fuerit sic obtentum; diversae enim sunt professiones."

The very particular custom was that according to which judgment was passed in doubtful issues, or that which induced a presumption in line with which judgment was passed (*cui statur*), unless perchance the contrary could be proved.[23]

This last species of custom gave rise to some interesting conclusions. The first was that to the mind of Hostiensis the community or group of the narrowest extension still capable of inducing a legal custom had to be one in which a legal problem involving a judicial procedure could arise. He did not point to any further species (the *consuetudo valde specialissima*) in accordance with which a legal custom could obtain, for instance, for a family circle, or among children, or with reference to recreational pursuits. For him an established custom stood for law, and before any such custom could be operative in the nature of law it had to involve a legal problem which at the same time related to a common good.

Again, from the wording which accompanied the discussion of Hostiensis in relation to the *specialissima consuetudo,* one may conclude that he regarded the judge bound to issue his sentence in line with the custom (*cui statur*) according to the presumption it induced, unless that presumption had to yield to contrary furnished proof. The problem whether it was the people along with the sanction of the legislator who induced a custom that had the force of law, or whether it was the judgment rendered *in contradicto* which lent to a material custom the force of law, vexed the commentators quite persistently. Hostiensis refrained from giving a definitive answer. For in the passage just treated he seemed to make the judge dependent upon the custom in a doubtful matter, but in another passage, wherein he defined custom, he stated that it was *induced* by means of a judgment rendered *in contradicto* along with the general *co-approval* of its users:

> Consuetudo est . . . contradictorio iudicio inductus, communi utentium comprobatione.[24]

---

23. "Item est specialissima secundum quam in dubiis iudicatur, et hoc praesumptionem inducit, cui statur, nisi forte contra probetur." —*loc. cit.*

24. Rubricam in Lib. I, tit. 4, *de consuetudine,* n. 1.

It remained for later commentators to resolve this problem of the rôle of the judge in bringing to a custom the force of law. However, Hostiensis in his *Summa* did re-emphasize the cardinal principle that a binding custom is on a par with law. Two particular instances wherein he cited the Roman Law in order to give prominence to this principle may here be adduced as proof of the statement.

In Lib. I, tit. 4, *de consuetudine*, n. 12, where Hostiensis treated of the *specialissima consuetudo,* he employed the words, *Consuetudo legem imitatur,* in evident reliance upon the text contained in Inst. (1, 2) 9, to which he specifically referred. Again, in Lib. IV, tit. *de agricolis,* n. 4, where Hostiensis dealt with the custom, prevalent in certain places, of governing the disposal of the estate of a rustic, he contended that the custom of the place should be supported, *si praescripta sit,* for, as he added, *Consuetudo est optima legum et dubiorum interpres,* which statement reflects the content of D. (1, 3) 37.

In addition, Hostiensis embodied the phrase *condere legem* when he considered whether the people had the capacity of inducing a law. This phrase occurs in the following statement:

> Sicut minor pars populi non potest condere legem, sic nec consuetudinem inducere.[25]

At first glance it could appear that Hostiensis was unrealistic in assuming that any number of people in an ecclesiastical community could *establish a law.* But in the passage here quoted the commentator intended simply to teach that indeed the greater, but not the lesser, part of the people in a community could induce a custom. The use of the expression *condere legem* for the rounding out of the sentence was not the thing of importance in his statement. Hostiensis seemed simply to employ a phrase that was well known and understood among the canonists: it emphasized the sanction which as an inherent element of law was essential for the existence of a legal custom.

ARTICLE 5. *Ioannes Andreae (1272-1348)*

Ioannes Andreae, among the chief contributors to the *Glossa Ordinaria* on the *Liber Sextus,* wrote other works, the most valuable among

25. Hostiensis, *Summa,* Lib. I, tit. 4, *de consuetudine,* n. 6.

them being his *Commentaria Novella in Quinque Libros Decretalium.*[26] He has been called the "Father of Canon Law and Its Trumpet." He lived approximately between the years 1270 and 1348, remaining a layman all his life. This particular commentary on the *Decretals* of Gregory IX he completed around the year 1338, while teaching at the School of Bologna.[27]

Ioannes Andreae did a great deal toward clarifying thought on the principles of custom. He minimized the position of the judge in giving legal validity and force to custom; he drew a classic comparison between custom and law, and outlined their common attributes; and in a number of instances he placed qualifications on the proposition that only those communities which can establish law can induce a legal custom.

He professed his disagreement with the doctrine that a legal custom could evolve only upon a judgment rendered *in contradicto.* His statement follows:

> Consuetudo quae attenditur circa factum vel processum iudicis, et illa quae attenditur circa communia gesta hominum alicuius civitatis, castri, villae debet esse obtenta contradictorio iudicio, hoc non placet . . . quia sine iudice et iudicio potest quis sibi acquirere ius usu et consuetudine.[28]

Accordingly he did not regard the sentence of a judge as essential for the establishment of a legal custom. In proof of his statement Ioannes Andreae recounted a number of legal customs as found in ceremonial law, which had never been subjected to the decision of a judge.

Next he stressed the fact, in clear and striking passages, that custom and law depended on like factors for their existence. Thus he stated:

> Consuetudo imitatur legem . . . sicut autem lex civilis vel canonica debet esse iusta, honesta, possibilis quoad materiam, et certa et

26. The edition available to the writer is the one that appeared at Venice in 1581.

27. Cf. Van Hove, *Prolegomena,* pp. 474-475, and 479.

28. *Novella,* ad c. 11, X, *de consuetudine,* I, 4, n. 38.

> clara quoad formam . . . sic et consuetudo; alias incerta, obscura, et impossibilis non valebit.[29]

In this passage express mention was made of the juridical requisites for a valid custom. The rules there given are as applicable today as they were in the fourteenth century. A custom had to be in accord with justice, in harmony with the moral order, possible of fulfillment in respect to its matter, and definite and clear in respect to its form. It seems proper to relate these rules to the factor of the community's capacity for the inducing of a legal custom, since under the title on Custom as contained in the present-day *Code of Canon Law* there is no canon which with similar force sets custom and law on a parity basis. The enumeration of these rules, then, serves well to emphasize this cardinal principle.

A second statement of Ioannes Andreae on this parallel follows in the same passage of the *Novella:*

> Item conveniunt lex et consuetudo in causa finali. Sicut enim lex ad bonum publicum et communem utilitatem producitur, et fit ad informationem morum et decisionem casuum, et humanos actus regulat . . . sic et consuetudo.

This quotation pertains even more closely to the subject of this dissertation. Just as a valid law had to be directed essentially to the public good and to common usefulness (for order and peace in the community), so likewise custom. If there were no other statements of jurists by which to judge, and no discussion whether the community capable of inducing a legal custom was the *communitas capax inducendi legem* or the *communitas capax recipiendi legem,* this passage would give an insight into the fact that the community in question had at most to be a public body, subject to public authority, and in need of law to regulate its acts.

The more particular problem however, namely, which kind of community could induce a legal custom, was faced by Ioannes Andreae in a number of passages. In his very definition of custom he insisted that the community which instituted a custom had to be endowed with public authority:

---

29. Ad X, *de consuetudine,* I, 4, *addenda,* n. 13.

> Consuetudo est ius quoddam illius populi moribus institutum qui auctoritate publica ius condere potest.[30]

But in his further explanation of the concept of such a community (the *populi* as he called it), he unsuccessfully attempted to fuse the concepts of Canon and Roman Law, depending for the latter on the theory of the Roman jurist Julian:

> ... quia, sicut lex, consuetudo est vel fuit praeceptum populi... nil enim interest an verbis declaret populus voluntatem, an rebus istis et factis.
>
> *Populus* excludit consuetudinem privati vel patrisfamiliae, quae ius non inducit.[31]

Nevertheless, proof that Ioannes Andreae recognized the fact that the Church has its authority founded in a monarchical, and not in a popular or democratic, system is deducible from the following two particular passages:

> ... opponit Innocentius quod consuetudo praeiudicat iuri positivo, cum sit illius abrogatrix, interpretatrix et conditrix. A contrario, dicunt quidam secundum Innocentium quod consuetudo habebat hanc auctoritatem olim quando populus condebat legem; hodie secus, ex quo illa potestas translata fuit in principem.[32]
>
> Opponitur: illius est tollere legem positivum, cuius est inducere, vel sui maioris, minoris non. ... Sed lex communis, canonica vel civilis, inducitur a papa vel a principe: consuetudo autem insurgit ex actibus privatorum qui sunt minores; ergo ipsorum actus legem etiam positivam tollere non possunt.[33]

Ioannes Andreae admitted the validity of this argument in the question regarding the capacity of a provincial custom for the abrogation everywhere of the extant universal law—a small concession! But he staunchly defended the potential legislative capacity inherent in formative custom, though rather speciously, when he stated:

---

30. Ad X, *de consuetudine,* I, 4, *addenda,* n. 11.
31. Ad X, *de consuetudine,* I, 4, *addenda,* n. 6—cf. etiam D. (1, 3) 32.
32. Ad c. 11, X, *de consuetudine,* I, 4, n. 42.
33. Ad c. 11, X, *de consuetudine,* I, 4, n. 47.

> ... sed derogare possunt in eo regno, provincia, vel loco, ut sicut ibi legem municipalem facere possunt, sic et consuetudinem inducere. . . .[34]

However, he recaptured his genius of analysis in the last statement of this passage in which he declared:

> ... et tamen ad obiectionis solutionem fateri oportet, quod nec in loco id possent, nisi quia papa vel princeps id expresse permittit.[35]

The final passage to be cited from Ioannes Andreae is the one in which he categorized customs as public and private, indicated by what agency each was induced, and then pointed to what validity it had in law:

> Alii sic dividunt, quod consuetudo est aut publica aut privata. Prima dicitur ius quoddam eius moribus constitutum qui publica auctoritate ius condere potest.[36]

A public custom could be either general or particular. But in either case to be recognized as law it had to be brought into being through the practice of him who by reason of public authority was able to establish law. Whether or not Ioannes Andreae felt that a public custom to be law needed only to exist with the express sanction of the legislator or also in consequence of his active collaboration can hardly be discerned from this passage alone.

On the other hand, a private custom was one that was induced by a private party. It served to express the intention of the user and to gain for him a *ius quaesitum.*

> Privata vero dicitur alicuius verbi vel actus a privato frequentatio, et operatur hoc ad declarandum intentionem suam in verbis et factis a se probatis, vel gestis, vel ab alio pro ipso. Item dicitur ius ex privatis usibus ipsi utenti quaesitum.[37]

A private custom, then, seemed rather to achieve a status of legal prescription than a status of true law. From this it is evident, then, that Ioannes Andreae persisted in teaching that the practice of a community which was to be capable of inducing a legal custom had somehow to have the sanction of that public authority which had the power to estab-

34. *Loc. cit.*
35. *Loc. cit.*
36. Ad X, *de consuetudine,* I, 4, *addenda,* n. 19.
37. *Loc. Cit.*

lish true laws. There was as yet no express suggestion that a legal custom could be induced by a community, though it had but the simple capacity of receiving a law.

ARTICLE 6. *Panormitanus (1386-1453)*

The final pre-Tridentine commentator who will be discussed in this dissertation is Nicolaus de Tudeschis, commonly called Panormitanus. Born in 1386, he became a Benedictine monk, taught law in various places, held responsible posts at Rome in the confidence of the Supreme Pontiff, and died as Archbishop of Palermo in 1453.[38]

Panormitanus in his treatise on custom alleged for it an increasing importance in the fashioning of law.[39] Like Ioannes Andreae he had much to say about the tenuous rôle of the judge in sanctioning a custom. He reiterated the fact that a true custom is a law, and therefore must fulfill the requisites for a law if it is to have full legal worth. Finally, he restated indeed the proposition that the community which was capable of founding a law was the one that could induce a legal custom, but he added many interesting qualifications.

First, express evidence that custom was rising steadily to a singular place in the formation of law is found in this defense of it by Panormitanus. He declared:

> . . . quis gerens actum contra ius praetextu consuetudinis pravae, et quo adhuc gravitas consuetudinis non erat per prius declarata, non debet puniri tanquam legis transgressor, sed debet tolerari praetextu consuetudinis.[40]

And thus he furnished implicit evidence of his high regard for the worth of custom. He reduced to its proper proportions the rôle of the judge in approving a custom. He did not invest the judge with any arbitrary power of approving or disapproving a custom; he insisted that the judge could act only as an authorized interpreter of the law (with

---

38. Cf. Van Hove, *Prolegomena,* p. 497.

39. Nicolaus de Tudeschis (Abbas Panormitanus), *Commentaria* in Quinque Libros Decretalium (5 vols. in 7, Venetiis, apud Juntas, 1588), ad X, *de consuetudine,* I, 4.

40. Ad c. 7, X, *de consuetudine,* I, 4, n. 5.

customs being part of the body of law), and as one who gave public faith and acceptance to acts.

With respect to the judge's rôle as interpreter of the law, Panormitanus contended that, while a custom altogether unreasonable was null of itself, a custom which was unreasonable only in consequence of a law had first to be reprobated by a judge before it became ineffective as an agency of law.[41] He limited this power of reprobation in the judge by gauging it in accordance with the judge's legal position as a custodian of the law and as an arbiter of disputes respecting it, for he maintained that with respect to a custom opposed by a subsequent law the custom was to be reprobated only when its continued observance implied a serious burden for the Church.[42]

The judge's power of giving public faith and acceptance to a custom already induced, Panormitanus explained in his comment on the *Glossa's* sixth condition for a valid custom, *ut consuetudo sit obtenta in contradictorio iudicio:*[43]

> Fatentur tamen doctores utriusque iuris quod ex actu iudiciario introducitur consuetudo, puta, quia iudex iudicavit contra legem, populo sciente et non contradicente; unde actus iudicialis sufficit ad probandam consuetudinem, non ut actus iudicarius, sed quia per illum actum detegitur consensus populi.[44]

Thereupon he reiterated the fact that an approved custom stands as a law, and therefore in line with this legal status must fulfill the requisite for any law.

He illustrated the import of this fact excellently in a passage wherein he contrasted particular statutes and customs invoked against imperial civil law on the one hand, and particular statutes and customs established against canon law on the other. He contended that in the civil system secular persons could establish a law contrary to the law of the Emperor. The reason, he thought, was that in civil affairs the law had as its end the public good and utility for private persons, so that if the people wished to prejudice themselves by founding a contrary

---

41. Ad c. 1, X, *de consuetudine,* I, 4, n. 1.
42. *Loc. cit.*
43. Cf. *supra,* p. 13.
44. Ad c. 11, X, *de consuetudine,* I, 4, n. 16.

law the Emperor would not trouble himself over it. Inasmuch as customs differed among people, the Emperor wished persons to establish laws and legal customs for themselves, simply by way of their own prejudgment. But then he continued:

> Sed ius canonicum principaliter intendit hominem dirigere in Deum, et venit ad bonum publicum ecclesiasticum. Unde statutum contrarium editum ab inferioribus praesumitur temerarium et ambitiosum, et fini aeterno contrarium . . .; sed consuetudo toleratur quia surgit ex tacito consensu, *et non praesumit tantam ambitionem;* item, quia maius scandalum oritur ex consuetudinis reprobatione cum concurrat tacitus consensus, longo tempore continuatus.[45]

In another place, in dealing with the requisites for a valid custom, Panormitanus asked how it could be known that a custom was or was not reasonable. He replied: " . . . cum consuetudo consistat *in iure,* non habet pars probare ipsius rationabilitatem, sed iudex habet hoc discernere."[46]

Lastly, Panormitanus introduced a rectifying concept into the proposition that only the community which was able to establish law could also induce a formal custom. He began his treatment of custom in general with the definition of Ioannes Andreae: "Consuetudo est quoddam ius moribus illius introductum qui publica auctoritate legem condere potest."[47] But he immediately pointed out the flaw which was contained in this definition, for

> consuetudo potest induci contra canones per inferiores a Papa, et tamen inferiores non possunt edere legem, seu statutum, contra canones.[48]

He thereupon offered another definition, which revealed elements of a much more liberal concept. This definition was such that substantially it foreshadowed the doctrine now obtaining in the Church's Code of law:

45. Ad c. 11, X, *de consuetudine,* I, 4, nn. 8 & 9.
46. Ad c. 11, X, *de consuetudine,* I, 4, n. 5.
47. *Ad Rubricam,* X, *de consuetudine,* I, 4, n. 1.
48. *Loc. cit.*

> Consuetudo est quoddam ius quod est moribus, seu usibus, populi totius, vel maioris partis, initiatum et continuatum et constitutum, legis habens auctoritatem.[49]

However, he was not satisfied to let the matter rest with this definition. In a later passage he again dealt with the proposition which reserved the inducing of a legal custom to a group or a community which was capable of establishing a law. He concluded, by way of example, that this capacity or power did not rest with women:

> Nam consuetudo non potest induci nisi ab habentibus potestatem legis condendae. Ideo mulieres non possunt inducere consuetudinem, quia non possunt condere leges.[50]

He followed this statement with an explanation of the exercise of Papal authority in sanctioning a custom:

> Oportet te dicere quod ista consuetudo assumit vires, non solum ex tacito consensu virorum ecclesiasticorum, sed auctoritate Papae permittentis induci consuetudinem contra canones.[51]

And he further explained this Papal rôle in his comment on the requirement of the *Glossa,* namely, *quod consuetudo sit inducta, sciente illo qui potest ius condere.*[52] This explanation he gave as follows:

> . . . Ioannes tenet quod consensus Papae, seu scientia, non requiritur ad consuetudinem inducendam; alias raro vel numquam induceretur consuetudo. Et haec opinio videtur communior, et mihi placet; primo post istum textum qui solum requirit quod sit rationabilis et praescripta; item (per c. 1, *de constitutionibus,* I, 2, in VI°) ubi dicitur: censetur ignorare statuta et consuetudines locorum.[53]

In this paragraph, at least, one finds a clearer expression of the theory that competent ecclesiastical superiors may give legal sanction to customs simply by laying down *conditions in the law* which must be fulfilled if the usages in a community are to take on legal worth. This notion of *legal consent* given by superiors in the written law did a

49. *Loc. cit.*
50. Ad c. 11, X, *de consuetudine,* I, 4, n. 8.
51. *Loc. cit.*
52. Cf. *supra,* p. 14.
53. Cf. *supra,* p. 24.

great deal to relieve commentators of their uncertainty as to whether it was the community in which there was resident some legislative power, or simply the community for which the accepting of a law was possible, that could induce a legal custom.

In the centuries that preceded the Council of Trent one notes that there was a consistent employment of the Roman Law terminology, not only in the official documents, but also in the writings of the commentators. Despite this fact the theory of the Roman jurist Julian, namely, that all laws and legal customs obtained their force from the consent of the community, became all but completely abandoned. The continued use of the Roman Law terminology made it difficult indeed for the canonists to set forth clearly the principles which they recognized as consistent with the Canon Law. The task of bringing a clearer expression to these principles remained for the post-Tridentine authors. It was they who shaped a terminology that accommodated itself to the doctrine that was received into the present Code.

Chapter IV

SUAREZ (1548-1617) AND THE COMMENTATORS TO THE TIME OF THE CODE

Article 1. *Suárez and His Followers in the Seventeenth Century*

Any treatment regarding various theories on custom in Canon Law after the age of the Decretalists and before the present Code of Canon Law must headline the teaching of the Spanish Jesuit Francisco Suárez, who lived from 1548 to 1617, and whose *Tractatus de Legibus et Deo Legislatore* appeared in 1612.[1] An initial difficulty, however, in presenting the theory of Suárez must be mentioned. He dealt at once with civil and canon law in this tract, and at times it is uncertain if he meant his conclusions to apply with equal force to both systems. The writer's attempt to deduce his principles on the community able to induce ecclesiastical customs will be conditioned by this dual presentation.

Relative to this problem Suárez took note of the current doctrine thus:

> Unde communiter doctores asserunt solum populum qui potestatem habeat condendi leges posse consuetudinem inducere.[2]

Among those whom he cited as holding this opinion were Pope Innocent IV (1243-1254), Ioannes Andreae (+1348), Panormitanus (+1453), and his own Magister, Navarrus (1493-1586).[3]

Suárez himself preferred to adhere to the doctrine of Saint Thomas Aquinas, as presented in the Angelic Doctor's Ia IIae, q. 97, art. 3, ad 3um,[4] wherein Thomas distinguished two types of juridic communities. In the one case, if there was a collectivity of freemen (*libera multitudo*) who were able to legislate for themselves, then the consent of the whole people to observe something which a custom among them

1. Cf. Van Hove, *Prolegomena,* p. 467. All quotations from Suárez in this dissertation will be taken from his *Opera Omnia* (28 vols., Parisiis: Vivès, 1856-1861), Vol. VI, *Tractatus de Legibus et Legislatore Deo* (hereafter cited *De Legibus*).

2. *De Legibus,* Lib. 7, c. 9, n. 7.

3. *Loc. cit.*

4. Cf. *supra,* p. 25.

made clear was of greater import than the authority of the ruler. In the other case, if the collectivity did not possess the unhampered power (*potestas libera*) of legislating for itself, then nevertheless a custom prevailing in such a group could obtain the force of law when it was tolerated by those to whom it belonged to impose a law on the group.

In his statement on this subject Suárez accepted the distinction of Saint Thomas. He wrote:

> Consuetudo legitima est vel populi liberi, et supremam potestatem habentis . . . vel est populi habentis pastorem, vel principem a quo regatur, et si consuetudo legitima, non sumitur tamquam populi acephali, sed ut coniuncti cum suo capite et habentis aliquo sufficienti modo influxum eius, vel per facultatem ad condendas leges municipales seu statuta, vel per approbationem consuetudinis aut iure ipso declaratam aut per tacitam voluntatem demonstratam.[5]

The type of community which retained supreme power for itself had in the mind of Suárez little if any relation to ecclesiastical law. He emphasized this attitude in another passage, where he stated:

> Praeterea sunt populi qui nullam habent facultatem statuendi, vel leges ferendi, etiam municipales, sed illas debent, vel a summo principe, vel saltem a propriis dominis vel pastoribus accipere; in hoc modo comparatur universa Ecclesia ad summum Pontificem, et omnes ecclesiae particulares ad suos Pastores; quia ad leges canonicas ferendas nulla est potestas in populo, nec in ipso clero sine suo capite et influxu eius, servata semper proportione, juxta varios modos legum et communitatum.[6]

Suárez insisted that, inasmuch as custom imitates true law, the community inducing a custom must have a capacity for legislative power. But he distinguished between communities which either *in actu* or *in potentia* were capable of legislating for themselves. A statement to this effect follows:

> Et ideo etiam considerate dixi . . . requiri communitatem quae sit capax potestatis legislativae, quia non est necessarium ut actu

5. *De Legibus,* Lib. 7, c. 13, n. 4.
6. *Ibid.,* c. 8, n. 3.

> illam habeat, quia per licentiam seu tacitum consensum principis suppleri potest.[7]

And in a further philosophical analysis he offered the following statement, particularly of ecclesiastical communities:

> Potest communitatem populi, de se et sola natura rei spectata, capacem esse potestatis legislativae etiam in materia religionis et divini cultus, et ideo, licet nunc in Ecclesia haec potestas elevata sit ad superiorem ordinem, et Pastoribus Ecclesia fuerit commissa, nihilominus de consensu eorumdem Praelatorum Ecclesiae permitti populis ut sua consuetudine possint obligari in tali materia cum tacito consensu eorumdem Praelatorum.[8]

In this passage Suárez seemed to be rationalizing the fact that communities within the Church, though not in the possession of any legislative power, nevertheless did induce legal customs. It would have been just as easy to explain why particular customs could not be induced by a non-legislative Church body if *de facto* they had never been induced and never had been permitted as a possibility. But accepting the state of affairs as they existed, he explained with good reason the fitness of the situation. He saw within the universal Church many communities of persons which *de se et sola natura rei spectata* were of social stability and accordingly needed a lawmaking power in the regulation of their affairs. Though in the divine plan of things most of these communities were denied the power to write laws for themselves, yet they had the capacity for this power, and with the consent of the proper authority they could activate this power by inducing legal customs.

In particular, then, Suárez asked the express question, "A qua communitate possit consuetudo introduci?" and he answered:

> ...ab illa quae sit capax potestatis legislativae pro seipsa, vel saltem sufficiens ut vera lex illi imponi potest.[9]

If one could validly apply these requisites to the communities of the Church (prescinding from civic communities of which Suárez was also writing), one had to conclude that those ecclesiastical communities

7. *Ibid.*, c. 9, n. 6.
8. *Ibid.*, n. 10.
9. *Ibid.*, n. 6.

were *actively* capable of legislative power which had within them an ecclesiastical legislator. Inasmuch as such communities were ruled by laws proper to themselves, they could induce customary law with the consent of the legislator. Further, other church communities were *passively* capable of legislative power in the measure at least that true law could be imposed upon them.

Suárez did not demand that a community be *de facto* regulated by its own laws before it could have a capacity for inducing legal customs. He demanded only that the community have a capacity for law.

> Dico autem necessariam illam capacitatem quia non potest forma introduci nisi in subjecto capaci, et ita suo modo non potest ius spiritualis consuetudinis (ut sic dicam) introduci nisi in subjecto capaci legis ecclesiastici.[10]

The conditions necessary that a community have a capacity for law can be drawn from various passages in the writings of Suárez. He alleged that the acts of the community inducing a custom must be *public*, and therefore the community itself must be public.[11] He also demanded that the acts inductive of a custom have a relation to the *common utility*, since a legal custom must have obligatory force even as does the law.[12]

In another place Suárez expressly stated that a community may be considered to have a capacity for law when "illa censeatur communitas *aliquo modo integra* et *perfecta* in (ecclesiastico) ordine."[13] When he demanded that for the inducing of a legal custom the community be *aliquo modo integra*, he seemed to mean that it be not *acephala*,[14] and more positively that "cum illa concurrat capitis consensus."[15] He employed the other term *perfecta* to denote that the community must have a capacity for legislative power. The sole contrasting example he offered of an imperfect community was the family.[16] Post-Code commentators without exception quote from Suárez in defense of their

10. *Ibid.*, n. 10.
11. *Ibid.*, c. 1, n. 8.
12. *Ibid.*, c. 3, n. 6.
13. *Ibid.*, c. 9, n. 10.
14. *Ibid.*, c. 8, n. 4.
15. *Ibid.*, c. 9, n. 10.
16. *Ibid.*, c. 3, n. 8.

views, and in this offer a number of different interpretations of the force of the word *perfecta.* The writer prefers at this point simply to present the doctrine of Suárez without interpretation.

Suárez did not admit any possibility of debate on the necessity of the consent of the legislator whenever there was question of the inducing of a legal custom by a community that did not possess the strict right of legislating for itself. He declared:

> . . . primum omnium statuendum est consensum principis in consuetudine introducenda necessarium esse.[17]

However, in a theory which remains the common opinion today he gave very clear expression to the mode of consent necessary on the part of the competent legislator. He stated that one mode of consent is called *personal,* and this may be either spoken (eliminative of the necessity of prescription) or tacit. The other mode of consent is called *legal,* and this is incorporated into the written law.[18]

Of legal consent he wrote:

> Quia si princeps statuit legem, ut consuetudo habens illas vel illas conditiones valeat, ex tunc consentit, et in particulari applicatur ille consensus ad similes consuetudines quando introducuntur in virtute illius legis.[19]

This notion of legal consent as one already supplied in the law is of great help, for in the light of it one may discuss the community able to receive ecclesiastical law without constantly adverting to the competent ecclesiastical superior whose consent is essential to the worth of any law, written or customary.

Suárez shed additional light on his position relative to the community capable of inducing a custom by pointing out some groups that lacked the needed qualifications.

1) The private practice of one person or of a family could not induce customary law, for before a practice could lead to a legal custom

17. *Ibid.,* c. 13, n. 1.
18. *Ibid.,* n. 6.
19. *Loc. cit.*

it had to arise from the whole community or from the greater part thereof. A practice induced by one person could rather be called a *ius dominii,* having preceptive, but not legal value.[20]

2) A private custom of an imperfect community, *quae legem ferre non potest,* as, for example, a private household, could not gain the force of law. It was only a pact among the members, implying at most the force of a dominative precept.[21]

3) Finally, those universal usages and traditions which constituted the *ius gentium* were not in the strict sense customs; rather, they were to be regarded as particularizations of the natural law. They were not really introduced, since they were perennially acknowledged. They were as imperative in their nature and existence as the natural law itself. They did not arise to supply any deficiency in the law.[22]

On the other hand, Suárez also listed various species of communities able to induce legal customs, for example, communities of clerics and of nuns (*moniales*).[23] He acknowledged the same capacity in communities of the laity, an example of this being a community of merchants. Of these latter he wrote:

> Nam communitas mercatorum, verbi gratia, eo modo potest consuetudinem introducere quo est capax legis; . . . si per se spectetur, sola potest condere statuta conventionalia, non proprias leges; si autem consideretur ut coniuncta principi, vel habens facultatem ab illo, potest facere statuta quasi-municipalia.[24]

In summarizing the doctrine of Suárez, then, one may present it thus: He held that a legal custom could be induced by a community which was *aliquo modo integra,* or which acted with the consent of a competent superior, and not acephalously; and which was *perfecta* in that it had legislative capacity, if not actively, then at least passively, in that laws could be imposed upon it.

Another author of the seventeenth century, Agostino Barbosa (1589-1649), treated of custom *ex professo,* as Suárez had done, but

20. *Ibid.,* c. 1, nn. 8 & 9.
21. *Ibid.,* c. 3, n. 8.
22. *Ibid.,* n. 7.
23. *Ibid.,* c. 9, n. 8.
24. *Ibid.,* n. 11.

the tract was much less exhaustive.[25] After stating that custom is in no way able to abrogate divine law, whether positive or natural,[26] he added that the same is not true of custom which forms against human law. He explained:

> . . . talis enim contra legem humanam admittitur, et valet dummodo rationabilis et praescripta sit. . . . Probatur ratione, etenim cum leges generaliter constituantur, et uti tales non possint semper variis locis, temporibus, ac personis convenire, recte fit ut prudenter a legislatoribus fuerit concessum, ut si quis populis a lege sibi non conveniente dissentiret, et illud contraria consuetudine induceretur, eadem vinceret et abrogaret talem legem.[27]

Though he did not cite Suárez in support of any of his arguments, he seemed to accept the doctrine that communities, even if simply capable of receiving a law, could nevertheless induce a legal custom. He regarded as a duly qualified community even a single family, hardly a legislative body, and for this he cited as his authorities both Menochius (+1607) and Velasco (+1665):

> . . . requiritur consensus saltem tacitus totius populi aut maioris partis . . . aut unius familiae, a qua posse consuetudinem introduci tenuerunt Menoch., Velasc., etc. . . .[28]

Though this passage probably referred to a custom induced in civil law, it was exceptionally liberal, and it leads one to believe that Barbosa certainly accepted the theory of Suárez, namely, that in Canon Law even the community upon which a law could simply be imposed had the capacity of inducing legal customs if there acceded the consent of the legislator.

Pirhing (1606-1679), who wrote around 1672, divided customs after the manner of Hostiensis,[29] but he followed Suárez, his fellow Jesuit, in all that he wrote on the subject.[30]

---

25. Cf. Barbosa, *Collectanea Doctorum in Ius Pontificum Universum* (6 vols., Lugduni: Brode et Arnaud, 1669), Lib. I, tit. 4, *de consuetudine.*

26. Barbosa, *op. cit.*, Lib. I, tit. 4, *Summarium*, n. 10.

27. *Loc. cit.*

28. Barbosa, *op. cit.*, Lib. I, tit. 4, c. 11, nn. 19 & 20.

29. Cf. *supra*, pp. 26-27.

30. Pirhing, *Ius Canonicum in V Libros Decretalium* (ed. novissima, 4 vols., Dilingae, 1722), Lib. I, tit. 4, *passim.*

ARTICLE 2. *Commentators Not in Accord with Suárez*

The theory of Suárez, namely, that also the community which was capable at least of receiving a law could likewise induce a legal custom, gained a larger share of approval than of disapproval after his own age. But there were commentators who, if they did not disagree with him expressly, nevertheless were so vague in their own views that they generally succeeded in raising doubts on the exact type of community capable of inducing a legal custom.

Fagnanus (1598-1678), the blind canonist of the seventeenth century and the *magnus rigoristarum princeps*,[31] flatly disagreed with Suárez' theory regarding custom. But his opposition hinged on the type of consent necessary for a custom on the part of him who can establish written law rather than on the persons who by their acts induce the custom. For in one place he wrote, "Consuetudo laicorum non obstringit clericos," and thus implicitly acknowledged the fact that the laity to whom legislative power was regularly not granted in the Church could nevertheless induce a custom which acquired a binding force.[32]

Elsewhere he made the following statement: "Intantum valet consuetudo inquantum nititur tacito consensu eius qui potest ius condere."[33] This thought he developed expressly against the opinion of Sanchez (1550-1610) and Suárez:

> Nec satis est... scientia illa generalis... sed requiritur specialis et individua [here he cited a number of Rotal decisions in support of his argument]. Quinimmo, nec sufficit consensus Principis permittentis, sed requiritur etiam approbantis, cum eadem potestas requiratur in legis abrogatione quae requiritur in eius editione.[34]

De Luca (1614-1683), writing shortly after Fagnanus, reviewed the ancient origin of customs in the law. He admitted that originally all

31. Cf. Van Hove, *Prolegomena*, p. 537.

32. Fagnanus, *Commentarium in V Libros Decretalium* (4 vols., Venetiis, 1696), ad c. 1 (*Consuetudines*), *de consuetudine*, Lib. I, tit. 4, n. 39.

33. Fagnanus, *op. cit.*, ad c. 8, *de consuetudine*, Lib. I, tit. 4, n. 28.

34. Fagnanus, *op. cit.*, ad c. 1 (*Utrum autem*), *de cognatione spirituali*, Lib. IV, tit. 11, n. 18.

power to make laws was vested in the people, who only gradually entrusted the power to a ruler. Accordingly he stated that in certain instances the people could reassume their ancient right by inducing a custom which would have binding power.[35]

However, in another passage he seemed rather to move to the side of Fagnanus:

> Unde quemadmodum dicta communitas, eiusque populus id statuere non posset quia communitatibus Superiorem recognoscentibus, tam de iure communi, quam fortius in statu Ecclesiastico . . . non conceditur statuere contra ius . . . idcirco neque consuetudo desuper induci potuit, quia quod fieri non potest expresse, minus tacite fieri potest . . . nisi ageretur de immemorabili, quo casu neque operativa esset, tamquam lex ab eo tacite ordinata, sed potius tamquam privilegium Supremi Principis ad id potestatem habentis.[36]

Devoti (1744-1820), whose treatise on church law appeared at the very beginning of the nineteenth century, bypassed all lengthy discussion regarding the type of community capable of inducing a legal custom. He chose to incorporate the theory of the Romanist Julian[37] on the real origin and force of custom. In consequence he wrote:

> Consuetudinis ius est inductum populorum moribus, et usu diuturno; nam lex humana ab hominum voluntate procedit, neque interest, num ea verbis an factis declaretur . . .; unde oritur consuetudo quae vim legis habet.[38]

If Devoti had pursued this thought to its logical outcome, he would in all probability have concluded that only those persons whose will made law in an ecclesiastical polity, or who had the power to establish law, could induce a legal custom.

Phillips (1804-1872), a German canonist and a convert to the Church, was among the foremost commentators of the nineteenth cen-

---

35. De Luca, *Theatrum Veritatis et Justitiae* (15 vols. in 9, Coloniae Agrippinae, 1706), I, *De Hereditate*, Disc. XXIII, n. 7.

36. De Luca, *op. cit.*, XV, *De Regalibus*, Disc. LXXVII, n. 2.

37. Cf. *supra*, p. 2.

38. Devoti, *Tractatus Iuris Canonici Universi* (3 vols., Romae, 1803-1815), Lib. I, tit. 16, n. 5.

tury on the general treatise of custom.[39] He, too, took a strict view regarding custom in its potential adverse influence relative to the common law. For example, he limited rather severely the possibilities of legal customs against the law, favoring much more those which as outside the law made up for the *lacunae* in the written law.[40]

Taking a stand against those who were ready to grant a certain autonomy to most of the communities in the Church as far as the inducing of legal customs was concerned, he stated:

> Très souvent ces sortes d'usages se presentent sous la forme d'observances speciales à telle ou telle corporation religieuse, investie du droit d'autonomie, . . . mais cette théorie n'est pas admissible, attendu qu'il existe un grand nombre de coutumes entièrement étrangères a cette sorte d'autonomie.[41]

De Angelis (1824-1881), like some of the other authors cited in this article, gave only a scanty treatment to the subject of custom as an agency of law in the Church. In his doctrine he adhered to rigorous standards. He left room for a rather comprehensive enumeration of customs which as a baneful blight could make inroads on the very marrow of ecclesiastical discipline. On this point he commented as follows:

> Et hic notandum verba "disrumpere nervum ecclesiasticae disciplinae" significare praecipue attenuationem directam auctoritatis iudicis ecclesiastici vel praelati.[42]

We may appraise his general attitude from a caution which he furnished for the guidance of communities in the matter of inducing customs:

> . . . non est enim lex nisi a superiore, et populus non posset suis moribus legem efformare, sed magis mores suos componere exactos ad legem, quam a superiore recepit.[43]

---

39. Cf. Wehrlé, *De la Coutume*, ch. VII.

40. Phillips, *Du Droit Ecclesiastique* (traduit par J. P. Crauzet, 2. ed., 3 vols., Paris: Le Coffre, 1833), III, 419 ff.

41. Phillips, *op. cit.*, III, 395.

42. De Angelis, *Praelectiones Iuris Canonici* (5 vols. in 9, Romae: Della Pace, 1877-1891), Lib. I, tit. 4, *de consuetudine*, n. 6.

43. *Ibid.*, n. 10.

ARTICLE 3. *Commentators of the Eighteenth Century in Accord with Suárez*

Reiffenstuel (1642-1703) followed Suárez very closely in his treatment of custom. But he emphasized the fact that an imperfect community, or one that was governed only by precept, was incapable of inducing a legal custom in view of its instable existence and uncertain duration, inasmuch as the precepts expired upon the death of the preceptor. To the question, "Per quos possit vel non possit induci consuetudo?", he supplied the following answer:

> ... non ab una tantum persona, neque ab aliqua communitate imperfecta, inquantum eorum praecepta expirant morte praecipientis.[44]

In his enumeration of the various categories of legal custom he retained the territorial division employed by Hostiensis *generalissima, generalis, specialis,* and *specialissima,* and likewise explained each division after the manner of Hostiensis.[45] He also included a persuasive paragraph on the reason that supported the legal force of custom in Church law. He declared:

> ... quia lex tota ordinatur ad bonum commune subditorum, si longa experientia, optima rerum magistra, constet, legem sive canonem a subditis non observari, sicque eam non esse moribus hominum accomodatam, imo potius deservire ad laqueum conscientiarum, quam ad utilitatem subditorum; tum ea a legislatore, subditorum infirmitati condescendente, censetur per consensum saltem tacitum, atque legalem, denuo revocari.[46]

Schmalzgrueber (1663-1735), a ranking author of the eighteenth century, agreed with Suárez on the generic type of community capable of inducing a legal custom, but he approached the subject with great caution. He stated:

---

44. Reiffenstuel, *Ius Canonicum Universum* (5 vols. in 7, Parisiis: Vivès, 1864-1870), Lib. I, tit. 4, n. 110.

45. Reiffenstuel, *op. cit.,* Lib. I, tit. 4, nn. 14-17.

46. *Ibid.,* n. 4.

> Dubium est, an consuetudinem quae vim legis habeat, introducere possit populus superiorem recognoscens, et non habens auctoritatem condendi legem.... Ratio dubitandi est quia talis communitas non habet potestatem condendi legem, quippe quae residet penes superiorem illius.
>
> Sed respondendum est affirmative. Clarum est de consuetudine abrogante legem; nam ad hanc introducendam sufficit esse communitatem cui lex imponi possit. Maior difficultas esset de consuetudine constitutiva novae legis . . . sufficit autem ad consuetudinem introducendam, quae vim legis habet, quod illa communitas, quae talem consuetudinem introducit, *de se* possit ferre legem, et accedat consensus legalis principis.[47]

Upon stating that it was necessary for the greater part of the community which induced the custom to have given its consent, he added that the members of the community had to be persons who were capable of subjection to law:

> Haec maior pars debet esse ex personis habilibus et capacibus legis: unde amentes, et infantes, et omnes illi, qui legibus non tenentur, non possunt sua consuetudine legem abrogare, aut novam constituere.[48]

While this note was not original with Schmalzgrueber,[49] he stated it concisely, and it was an important factor to note in an analysis of the community capable of inducing a legal custom.

Böckhn (1690-1752), a highly respected commentator of the eighteenth century, defined in a different manner the division of custom according to communities. His first division contemplated public custom, which related directly to the public status of the Church, and private custom, which referred to the status of private individuals. His second division looked to the absolutely general custom, which was received throughout the entire Church, to the relatively general custom which obtained throughout a large province, and, finally, to the par-

47. Schmalzgrueber, *Ius Ecclesiasticum Universum* (5 vols. in 12, Romae, 1843-1845), Lib. I, tit. 4, n. 3 (hereafter cited as Schmalzgrueber).

48. Schmalzgrueber, Lib. I, tit. 4, n. 14.

49. Cf. Suárez, *De Legibus*, Lib. VII, c. 9, n. 14.

ticular or local custom, which was observed in a particular or local community, for example, in a city.[50]

The "perfect community," as treated by Saint Thomas and Suárez, he defined thus:

> ... ita ex pluribus familiis, aut personis, constat, ut in statu Ecclesiastico vel politico considerationem habeat, ac speciali regimine boni communis causa dirigatur; ut sunt Ecclesia universalis, regnum, provincia, civitas, municipium, Ordo Religiosorum, exercitus militaris, etc.[51]

This was the type of community for which laws were passed, and it was similar communities that could induce legal customs.[52] He added curias and collegiate bodies to his list of perfect communities,[53] and seemed ready, in reliance upon the opinion of Schmier (1680-1728), to leave room also for the inclusion of an illustrious family whose members and descendants were welded together as a social unit. As a matter in which this last community might induce a legal custom he pointed to the matter of succession *ab intestato.*

ARTICLE 4. *Commentators of the Nineteenth Century in Accord with Suárez*

Bouix (1808-1870), who furnished a very methodical treatment of the whole field of custom, drew heavily from Suárez for his opinions. His definition of the community capable of inducing a custom is a combination of that of Suárez and of Reiffenstuel. He wrote:

> ... ponunt ab ea communitate posse induci consuetudinem cui potest imponi lex; cum lex sit commune praeceptum, obligans etiam post mortem legislatoris atque in perpetuum, sicque non nisi communitati perfectae imponi valeat.[54]

---

50. Bőckhn, *Ius Canonicum Universum* (3 vols., Salisburgi, Parisiis, 1776), Lib. I, tit. 4, nn. 10-11.

51. *Ibid.,* tit. 2, n. 35.

52. Bőckhn, *ibid.,* tit. 4, n. 27.

53. *Loc. cit.*

54. Bouix, *Tractatus de Principiis Juris Canonici* (3. ed., Parisiis, 1882), p. 357.

The examples of this type of community which he offered were the clerics and the people of one diocese, of one province, of a region of provinces; and, again, the religious of all the convents of an Order.[55]

Among legal customs he distinguished, on the one hand, custom properly so called, which arises from a perfect community, and, on the other hand, the *stylus curiae* analogous to custom, which exists "ad significandum ordinem consuetum in judiciis procedendi, et instrumenta conficiendi quae ad judicia respiciunt."[56] He declared that if a certain practice in judicial matters arose solely from usage and the procedure always continued the same, then such a *stylus curiae* could be considered a species of customary law.

Bouix explained in the following way the jurisprudence attaching to the right of a community to induce a legal custom. Just as a legislator may delegate his power to make laws, so through a general decree he may establish that customs will have legal force if they be fortified with the conditions that he demands.[57]

Bauduin (1860-1942), who wrote a doctoral dissertation on custom in general, included the subject of this dissertation in quite some detail. He gave some space to explaining the term *observantia,* and distinguished it from custom strictly so called. If the observance was no more than a pact among members of an imperfect community, it could become only a *ius conventionale,* and not a *ius consuetudinarium,* which latter alone implied a legal right.[58]

He taught that there are some moral bodies in the Church to which either through the common law, through privilege, or through the agency of legal prescription there pertains a certain autonomy in carrying on negotiations within their own sphere of action. If these communities have the power of establishing laws or statutes for themselves expressly, they can also do this tacitly through expressing their consent by means of their actions. And if these actions can be called an *observantia,* then it is licit to call the effect of this observance a particular species of customary law. However, it must always be determined in

55. *Loc. cit.*

56. *Op. cit.,* p. 353.

57. *Op. cit.,* pp. 382 ff.

58. Bauduin, *De Consuetudine in Iure Canonico* (Lovanii, 1888), p. 6.

each case whether what is called an observance is only a fact or has taken on legal force.[59]

Bauduin adopted the theory of Suárez, namely, that the "perfect" community which is capable at least of receiving law can alone induce a legal custom. He distinguished the "perfect" community in this sense from the self-sufficient and self-contained society "quae simul cum fine in suo ordine completo habet omnia media necessaria ad illum finem assequendum."[60] This latter constituted the perfect society in an absolute sense. He explained his thought and doctrine as follows:

> Fieri vero potest ut societas de se imperfecta ab altera, cuius pars est, sibi habitualiter communicata habeat media, quae natura sua soli societati perfectae competant; tunc huiusmodi societas dicitur perfecta non absolute, sed relative ad alias: exempla sunt dioeceses et ordines regulares. . . .[61]

The communities which had the power to establish law could certainly induce a custom. But Bauduin was ready to predicate the same prerogative for the relative "perfect" community:

> Quinimmo societates, quae natura sua non sunt incapaces vel recipiendi potestatem legislativam a societate perfecta, etsi actu eam non receperint; vel etiam recipiendi effectum huius potestatis, seu legem, dicuntur perfectae comparative ad alias societates in hoc ordine incapaces.[62]

Thus, Bauduin's definition of the community capable of inducing a legal custom was in full accord with that of Suárez, and it shed some further light on the condition which Suárez stressed, namely, that the community be "*perfecta in aliquo ordine.*"[63]

Belorgey, a contemporary of Bauduin, instituted still another division with reference to the communities capable of inducing a legal custom. He stated that one could regard a community either as local or as personal — local, if it was circumscribed by definite and real boun-

---

59. *Loc. cit.*
60. *Op. cit.*, p. 44.
61. *Op. cit.*, p. 45.
62. *Loc. cit.*
63. Cf. *supra*, p. 41.

daries, as in the case of a city, a diocese, or a kingdom; and personal, if the community's extension was determined through the factor of its membership, as in the case of a religious Order or a confraternity. He added:

> In utroque enim casu dari potest vinculum morale quoddam, regimen perfectum, ideoque communitas perfecta.[64]

He further stressed the fact that it was not of the essence of law or of custom that the law or custom bind all in the community. He declared that one part of a community to the exclusion of every other part of it could be in need of a particular regulation in a specific locality by reason of some condition prevailing there alone. A law, and therefore also a custom, was in such a case valid if it had the note of stability and proceeded from the same political authority that looked to the general good order of the community.[65]

Finally, in his acceptance of the theory of Suárez that the community which was capable of at least receiving a law could induce a legal custom,[66] he discussed the possibility of a single parish as qualifying in this regard. At first he seemed hesitant to commit himself on this point. But he concluded from the argument outlined in the paragraph above that not improbably a parish also enjoyed this capacity in a matter of lesser gravity and particularly after a very long usage.[67]

Wernz (1842-1914) furnished a good summary of the doctrine of Suárez relating to the subject of this dissertation. He furthermore set the stage for a fuller appreciation of the doctrine now contained in canon 26 of the Code. In listing the various categories of customs he employed the time-honored division of Hostiensis, and then offered the traditional reflections on each of them.[68] He declared his doctrine in the following clear and precise statement:

---

64. Belorgey, *De Consuetudine* (Locogiaci: Abbatiae St. Martini, 1893), p. 45.

65. *Op. cit.*, p. 46.

66. *Op. cit.*, p. 44.

67. *Op. cit.*, pp. 50-51.

68. Wernz, *Ius Decretalium* (2. ed., 6 vols., Romae et Prati, 1906-1913), I, n. 187.

Consuetudo . . . procedat necesse est a communitate, vel saltem a maiore illius parte quae legis ecclesiasticae recipiendae capax est; v. g., provincia ecclesiastica, dioecesis, ordo religiosus, etiam moniales.[69]

---

69. *Op. cit.*, I, n. 190.

Chapter V

CUSTOMS OF PARTICULAR COMMUNITIES SANCTIONED BY THE ROMAN CURIA

An examination of certain specific decrees among the numerous decisions and rescripts of the various Sacred Congregations of the Roman Curia will shed light on the proper understanding of the community able to induce a legal custom. Though none of the decrees here cited could be regarded as true law, they furnished an interpretation of the law as representing the mind of the legislator. Each selection will be presented under the headings of *species facti* and *species iuris* along with a few added comments of importance to the subject of this dissertation under the heading *attendenda.* The selections will be arranged according to the territorial extension of the community which induced the custom, from the most comprehensive to the least extensive.

ARTICLE 1. *National and Provincial Customs*

1) On February 16, 1867, the Sacred Congregation of the Council resolved the following doubt:

Species facti — The canons of a collegiate chapter in the country of France claimed a right in customary law to administer the last sacraments and to conduct the funeral of any canon of their chapter, even when he had residence outside of their parochial limits. In this particular case the pastor of the parish in which the canon had domicile claimed that the right was his by the written law.

Species iuris — The Sacred Congregation determined that this matter was the subject of a custom which, flourishing throughout France, gave to the collegiate chapter the above-mentioned rights over the canons of their college irrespective of their domicile.[1]

Attendenda — This question was settled on the foundation of a custom prevalent throughout a nation, in this case France. A custom will evidently be stronger the wider the extension of the custom.

1. S. C. C., 16 febr. 1867 — *Acta Sanctae Sedis* (41 vols., Romae, 1865-1908), III (1867), 127-133 (hereafter cited *ASS*).

2) On February 29, 1896, the Sacred Congregation of the Council resolved the following doubt:

Species facti — A group of Capuchins asked to be sustained in a custom of carrying their own cross in procession when a lay-member of their Order was being buried from a church not their own.

Species iuris — The Sacred Congregation sustained the custom after hearing the Procurator of the Order along with other sworn witnesses attest to the fact that this was the custom not in Sestre-Ponente alone where the dispute arose, but also throughout the province.[2]

Attendenda — The Sacred Congregation in the discussion of this case averred that this action was permissible not only to an Order, but also to a Confraternity, whenever a custom of the place had been induced. It spoke of the action as partaking more of the nature of a privilege than of customary law, though the rules for the inducing of a custom had been examined. There was a true juridic aspect to the case, since the greater number of priests attending the funeral from the Order gave to the obsequies a higher classification. Even in this light the custom was sustained. The Procurator of the Capuchins pointed to the extension of the custom throughout the province to give added strength to his petition.

ARTICLE 2. *Diocesan Customs*

1) On March 19, 1866, the Sacred Congregation of Bishops and Regulars resolved the following doubt:

Species facti — In an unnamed diocese in Italy there was called in question a very ancient custom whereby newly made beneficiaries had been relieved through the first half-year of their incumbency from paying the assessment for the repair of the cathedral.

Species iuris — The Sacred Congregation ruled that this custom had been reprobated in a Constitution of Benedict XIII, which had regulated this matter for Italy and the surrounding islands.[3]

Attendenda — As a rule, when a custom was declared null and void by the Roman Curia, the decision was founded in its irrational aspect.

---

2. S. C. C., 29 febr. 1896 — *ASS*, XXIX (1896), 80-88.
3. S. C. C. Ep. et Reg., 19 mart. 1866 — *ASS*, II (1866), 93-96.

Though no positive rule for the type of community able to induce a legal custom can in justice be drawn from this fact, one could form a legitimate prejudgment of liberality in approaching the matter. In this case the custom was not abrogated by reason of the community inducing it, for the diocesan beneficiaries whose tenure of incumbency had run less than a year had sustained the custom in law until the Constitution of Benedict XIII reprobated contrary customs.

2) On July 24, 1639, the Sacred Congregation of Rites was asked the following question:

Species facti — A group of exempt religious resident in the diocese of Ascoli Satriano requested approval of the custom of permitting religious to walk in procession in diocesan celebrations irrespective of a recent prohibition of the bishop.

Species iuris — The Sacred Congregation sustained the custom with the words, "*servari solitum quoad processiones.*"[4]

Attendenda — This custom had been induced *moribus clericorum exemptorum* throughout a diocese. The relations between religious and seculars in a locale often demanded regulation by law, and custom did much to define such law.

3) On August 3, 1765, the Sacred Congregation of the Council resolved the following doubt:

Species facti — A house of regulars within a certain parish in the diocese of Barcelona claimed this legal right by custom: on the feast day of Corpus Christi to receive the Blessed Sacrament in Its monstrance from the hands of the pastor after the Mass, to carry It in procession, and to return It to the pastor for Reposition.

Species iuris — The Sacred Congregation inquired of the bishop of the diocese for some verification of this custom. The bishop wrote:

> Ego ipse uno verbo EE. VV. respondeo quod in parochia et parochiis in quibus datur proprius parochus et pastor, qui sit presbyter saecularis, insolitum est et irregulare S. Sacramentum in processionibus quae fiunt in parochia differri ab alio quam a proprio parocho....

4. *Decreta Authentica Congregationis S. Rituum* (ab A. Gardellini collecta, cura H. Capalti edita, 3. ed., 4 vols., cum Supplementis usque ad annum 1888, Romae, 1856-1888), n. 1080 (hereafter cited *Decreta*).

The bishop concluded by saying that the alleged custom of the Regulars reflected a ridiculous claim and should be disregarded. The decision favored the proper pastor. It would have been illegitimate to allege that a custom had been induced in the one parish alone, since there was no concerted activity, but an attempted prescription of a personal right of the pastor. And there was no concordant activity in the diocese, as the bishop testified. Therefore the custom was rather judged a corruption than true law.[5]

Attendenda — It is often difficult to determine when a usage has been inductive of true law and when of a privilege. At times, however, the Roman Curia has abrogated an alleged custom for the reason that notoriously it was rather in the realm of the prescription of a personal right, as in this case. Again, however, inasmuch as certain groups did gain exemptions from the written law through the process of inducing a custom, the student is moved to make a prejudgment toward liberality in determining the *capax* community for inducing legal customs.

ARTICLE 3. *Customs Induced within a Diocese*

1) On April 28, 1888, the Sacred Congregation of the Council resolved the following doubt:

Species facti — In a few of the poor parishes in the diocese of Belluno it had been the custom to pay the Lenten preachers from the collection of the fourth Sunday of Lent, a collection taken to have Masses offered for the faithful departed. The laws governing the allocation of stipends aroused a doubt of conscience on the part of the pastors involved.

Species iuris — The Sacred Congregation ruled that the custom should be sustained. The common consent of the community of each of the churches could be presumed, since their greater good and utility was being served in the sermons of the Lenten preacher, otherwise unattainable.[6]

---

5. S. C. C., 3 aug. 1765 — *Thesaurus Resolutionum Sacrae Congregationis Conclii* (167 vols., Romae, 1718-1908), XXXIV, 127, *sub cap. Barchinonen* (hereafter cited *Thesaurus*).

6. S. C. C., 28 apr. 1888 — *ASS*, XXI (1888), 129-137.

Attendenda — This decision was made on the grounds of custom, though the reasons alleged could indeed seem somewhat tenuous. The consent of the parishioners in each of the parishes was presumed, since a greater good was derived from the existing practice, a consideration always applicable in customary law. Though indeed a number of the parishes of the diocese was subject to the same need in similar circumstances, each of the parishes seemed to have acted independently, so that one may conclude that a legal sanction was accorded to customs as established in the individual parishes.

2) On January 28, 1764, the Sacred Congregation of the Council resolved the following doubt:

Species facti — In the diocese of Viterbo in Italy there was a sodality chapel within the boundaries of a certain parish. One of the members of the sodality was buried from this chapel, and the pastor of the place demanded by right of custom more than the one-quarter share of the canonical stipend. The sodality refused to comply with the pastor's demand.

Species iuris — An investigation of the matter revealed that the custom as alleged by this pastor had arisen in other parishes of the diocese because of peculiar circumstances, v. g., in view of the tribute of honor paid by filial churches to their mother church, in consequence of the particular location of the burial ground, etc. The parish in question had not induced a similar custom; therefore the pastor of the place was not permitted to appropriate to himself the special legal right that attached to other parishes of the diocese through customary law.[7]

Attendenda — The proper distribution of stipends was a matter which needed regulation by law, in order that all rightful claimants might obtain their just share. The peculiar circumstances which determined the manner of this distribution could be limited to a very restricted territory, even to a single parish, as this response implied. However, for its enjoyment of a right in customary law the community, or those in it who were qualified to act in the particular case, needed to function in an active rôle for the inducing of the custom.

7. S. C. C., 26 ian. 1764 — *Thesaurus,* XXXIII (1764), 16.

3) On December 14, 1816, the Sacred Congregation of the Council resolved the following doubt:

Species facti — In a collegiate church in the town of Lavagna (near Genoa) a dispute arose between two canons over the right of precedence. D. Carabelli was made a canon in 1815 while already a priest. D. Gozzi was made a canon in 1809 while only a deacon. When D. Gozzi was ordained to the priesthood he demanded precedence in consequence of his seniority in the chapter, and this by right of customary law.

Species iuris — D. Gozzi defended his right in custom by citing a similar case in the cathedral chapter of the diocese, and by alleging a similar practice in another collegiate church of the diocese. But the Sacred Congregation refused him his petition on the grounds that

> . . . nec per unum aut alterum actum consuetudo inducitur, quae ut omnes norunt, ius quoddam moribus, scilicet actibus frequentatis institutum est.

Further, even if a custom prevailed in other collegiate chapters of the diocese, customs were not to become appropriated by one church from another even within the same diocese.[8]

Attendenda — The Sacred Congregation overruled the custom herein alleged solely on the score of the agency inducing the custom. First, it was made clear that a custom cannot legally be induced by one person of a community. Secondly, it was explained that the benefit which derives from a custom can be enjoyed only by those who with their acts actively contribute to the formation of the customary law. Finally, it was admitted that as long as the custom was rightly induced collegiate chapters could be regulated by customary law, since as a particular body within the structure of the Church they were in need of true law, which in the light of the peculiar circumstances and of the complex activities could be reflected through custom, which then stood as the best interpreter of the law.

---

8. S. C. C., 14 dec. 1816 — *Thesaurus*, LXXVI (1816), *sub cap. Albanen. Praecedentiae.*

4) On April 14, 1753, the Sacred Congregation of Rites was asked to resolve the following doubt:

Species facti — In the cathedral parish of Coimbra in Portugal there was question of the legitimacy of the custom of playing the organ on Saturdays of Lent and Advent when Solemn Votive Mass was sung in honor of the Blessed Mother.

Species iuris — The Sacred Congregation replied that the custom was to be sustained.[9]

Attendenda — This was a custom induced against the universal law, and therefore the local ordinary was unable to establish a particular law to sanction it. The practice was presented and treated as a custom, and thus was considered as having been induced through the common consent of the parishioners who acted in accord with their pastor in his public office. The factors relating to the extension of the community and to the common consent of the ones who engaged in the customary usage were in the case accepted as sufficient for endowing the usage with legal worth.

9. S. C. R., 14 apr. 1753 — *Decreta,* II, n. 4233.

CANONICAL COMMENTARY

PART II

THEORY ON THE COMMUNITY ABLE TO INDUCE LEGAL CUSTOMS

CHAPTER VI

PRELIMINARY NOTIONS

The canonical commentary on the subject of this dissertation is divided into two parts. The first part is devoted to an investigation of the essential notes which must attach to a community if it is to be considered capable of inducing legal customs. The second part is devoted to an application of these notes and the vindication of their validity as they relate to particular communities.

The starting point of this study is canon 26 of the Code, which states that the community able to induce a legal custom is that which is at least capable of receiving ecclesiastical law.[1] It is best immediately to define the terms employed in the canon, for they shall recur continuously in this work.

ARTICLE 1. *The Notion of Custom*

The word "custom" is used in popular speech to denote almost every form of habitual activity in which there has been some freedom of choice. But in an academic treatment of a phase of custom proper distinctions must be made. The word "usage" is a more apt generic term for what is popularly called "custom." Usage admits of division into observances, *stylus curiae,* traditions, customs of fact and customs of law. It is only the last two modes of usage in which this study interests itself.

An *observance* has been defined as a uniform mode of acting from which no legal obligation ensues.[2] The *stylus curiae* points simply to

1. Canon 26.—"Communitas quae legis ecclesiasticae saltem recipiendae capax est, potest consuetudinem inducere quae vim legis obtineat."

2. A. Van Hove, *Commentarium Lovaniese in Codicem Iuris Canonici,* Vol. I, Tom. III, *De Consuetudine et De Temporis Supputatione* (Mechliniae-Romae: H. Dessain, 1933), p. 7 (hereafter cited *De Consuetudine*).

the usually employed mode in the transcribing of acts of a juridical nature. Abbreviations and synopsized forms, as serving the convenience of the scribe, sufficiently manifest his mind in consequence of a usage in like matters.[3] *Traditions* in law refer to those statutes which indeed issued from a legislator, but which were preserved and maintained through the usages of the people.[4]

On the other hand, *custom,* viewed formally, denotes a community's consistent mode of acting that is vested with such conditions as to constitute a norm which with the sanction of public authority can become obligatory in character.[5] A custom remains *factual* the while it is in the process of being induced. It becomes *legal* (customary law) when there have been fulfilled all the conditions necessary that it be properly induced. When these conditions have been fulfilled, a custom, properly so called, will take on all the force of law.[6]

ARTICLE 2. *The Notion of a Community*

The notion contained in the word "community" is rather generic, and must be so defined as to permit of a number of subdivisions. The term "community" is evidently a term of contradistinction with reference to an individual person, i. e., for a community there must be a plurality of persons. The notion also demands some sort of unity in this plurality of persons, for otherwise there could be no communal note, no bond by which the members are drawn together. The word itself derives from two Latin words, *cum* and *unire,* which etymologically shape the definition of a community as "a plurality of persons united by a common bond." This definition gives to the notion of a "community" some similarity with two other terms with which it is *de facto* associated in the Code: the *coetus* and the *collegium.* A study

---

3. *Ibid.*, pp. 7 & 8.

4. *Ibid.*, p. 5.

5. *Ibid.*, p. 4.

6. Custom is also different from prescription. A single person or a group, considered as single and private persons, can by legal prescription acquire a *subjective right.* But a public group through repeated acts can regulate its common activities with the effect that they entail an obligatory force of *objective rights.* Prescription is subjective right, custom is objective right, or true law (cf. *supra*, p. 21, for the distinctions of Hostiensis).

of its relationship to these two terms can lead to a more concise definition.

The phrase, *communitati seu coetui,* is found in canon 73, § 4.[7] In this canon an obligation is placed on the community, *seu coetus,* of persons who enjoy a common privilege. The canon supposes that the privilege, when granted, was given to a unit of persons, distinguishable by reason of some common quality, however tenuous the union. The connotation of the canon seems to be that the similarity which exists between a community and a *coetus* is not one of identity, but rather one of likeness in which a distinction can still have its place.[8] It seems from the very force of the words that the notion of a community postulates a more readily distinguishable moral bond of unity among the persons composing it than the notion of a *coetus* postulates.

Communitas is used in a similar construction together with the word *collegium* in canon 2285, § 1.[9] In this case, too, a plurality of persons is postulated by both terms. However, the term *collegium* is correlated in Canon Law with the notion of a moral person.[10] But the collegiate moral person is constituted in the law for the purpose of according to a group of persons who are united for a common end the canonical status of one physical person, and then by a legal fiction the law views the moral person as an individual physical person, the subject of rights and duties.[11] The word "community" cannot be said necessarily to contain this legal notion of physical personality in its very definition. The context of canon 2285 makes this distinction even clearer.

---

7. "Nec ipsi communitati seu coetui integrum est renuntiare privilegio sibi dato per modum legis, vel si renuntiatio cedat in Ecclesiae aliorumve praeiudicium."

8. For the distinguishing force of the disjunctive *seu,* cf. A. Toso, *Ad Codicem Iuris Canonici . . . Commentaria Minora* (5 vols. — Vol. I, 2 ed., Taurini-Romae: P. Marietti, 1921), I, 77.

9. "Si communitas seu collegium clericorum delictum commiserit, suspensio ferri potest vel in singulas personas delinquentes vel in communitatem, uti talem, vel in personas delinquentes et communitatem."

10. Cf. canon 99.

11. Cf. Kilcullen, *The Collegiate Moral Person as Party Litigant,* The Catholic University of America Canon Law Studies, n. 251 (Washington, D. C.: Catholic University of America Press, 1947), who on p. 5 states: "This legal person, when duly constituted in law, becomes, like the natural person, a *subiectum iuris capax,* or capable of exercising rights and duties."

Rather than simply state that a *collegium clericorum* may be held *as one* for a delict which they have jointly committed, the canon employs the alternate word "community" to clarify the fact that each of the members of the college is to be considered as retaining his individuality, and therefore may be punished as an individual as well as with the community. While every collegiate body is a community, not every community is at the same time a collegiate moral person.

There are two further constructions in the Code which give insight into the notion of the word "community." In canon 717, § 2, it is stated that the patrimony of a confraternity or of a pious union, if it has been erected in a church not its own, or if its own church is at the same time a parish church, must be separated from the goods of the church or of the community (*a bonis fabricae vel communitatis*). Here the members of the parish are considered a community. Again, in canon 521, § 1, a house of women religious is referred to as a "community."[12]

Thus a community is in the Code considered to bear a similarity to a house of religious, to a parish, to a collegiate body, and to a mere *coetus*, or group. From these constructions its definition emerges as a plurality of persons, readily distinguishable as a moral unit by reason of a common bond, wherein nonetheless each member retains his individuality and is responsible for his individual actions.

One can hardly determine in every case how many persons must be united if through such a union they are to qualify as a community. If a collegiate body is in question, then at least three persons are necessary.[13] Reiffenstuel (1642-1703), when invoking a rule for determining notoriety in a delict, averred that it was sufficient if the major part of the community know of the delict, "dummodo in tali communitate non sunt pauciores homines quam decem."[14] This specific application he derived from a chapter in the *Decree* of Gratian in which was discussed the minimum number of persons that sufficed for the appointment of a pastor for them. Ten persons were there decreed as making a *populus*.[15]

---

12. "Unicuique religiosarum communitati detur confessarius extraordinarius qui quater saltem in anno ad domum religiosam accedat. . . ."

13. Canon 100, § 2.

14. *Ius Canonicum Universum*, Lib. V, tit. 1, n. 249.

15. Cf. c. 3, C. X, q. 3.

The existence of a community, given at least a minimum of three physical persons, will be more readily determined from the common bond uniting its members. The form of this common bond will derive from one or another of a number of circumstances. Vermeersch (1858-1936)-Creusen state that, though a community is as a rule distinguishable on the score of its territorial extension, the brand of unity is not necessarily always occasioned through this specific factor.[16] Michiels offers a threefold division of the potential bond of unity: territory, common vows or a multilateral contract, and common status or condition of life.[17] To repeat the definition of a community once again, it is a plurality of persons, readily distinguishable as a moral unit by reason of a common bond, wherein nonetheless each person retains his individuality and is responsible for his individual actions.

ARTICLE 3. *The Force of the Word* saltem

The word *saltem* in canon 26 indicates the settling of a historical controversy respecting the community able to induce a legal custom. In the historical synopsis of this work it has been shown that for ages commentators on the law had debated whether such a community was that in which there was resident some legislative power (*populus qui potest legem condere*[18] and *communitas capax potestatis legislativae pro seipsa*),[19] or that which was able simply to receive a law (*communitas cui saltem lex imponi potest*).[20] It is now clear that the community which is capable of receiving an ecclesiastical law may induce a legal custom — but in order to qualify the community must have this capacity at least. *A fortiori* the community in which there is legislative power may induce legal customs, since that is a more fully constituted form of community. The examination in this study of the kind of community that is able to induce legal customs will be conducted along this dual avenue of approach.

---

16. Vermeersch-Creusen, *Epitome Iuris Canonici* (3 vols., Vols. I-II, 6 ed., Mechliniae-Romae; H. Dessain, 1937-1940), I, 87.

17. Michiels, *Normae Generales Iuris Canonici* (2 vols., Lublin, Poloniae: Universitas Catholica, 1929), I, 142 (cited *Normae Generales*).

18. Cf. *supra,* p. 14.

19. Cf. *supra,* p. 40.

20. Cf. *supra,* p. 40.

ARTICLE 4. *The Force of the Word* capax

A community may induce a legal custom if it has the capacity for receiving an ecclesiastical law. The force of the word *capax* is explained in the statement of Suárez, *Forma non potest introduci nisi in subjecto capaci,*[21] a philosophical axiom, whose truth becomes evident upon the perusal of it. A gallon jug has a capacity for holding a gallon of liquid. A sieve of the same dimensions as a gallon jug has no capacity for holding any amount of liquid. The capacity of the jug will not vary with the amount of liquid actually within it. It may remain empty until it is shattered or be painted and used as an ornament, but its capacity for holding a gallon of liquid remains the while it exists.

Thus a community must have a capacity for law if it is to be able to induce a custom that obtains the force of law. Whether or not it is *de facto* regulated by its own laws is not the sole criterion of its capacity for law. Its capacity will be determined by the presence in the community of those elements which permit of its being regulated by law. What these elements are will be discussed, and the corresponding application will be made, in the following chapters.

ARTICLE 5. *The Notion of Law*

The classic definition of law is found in the writings of Saint Thomas. Law is "the regulation of right reason invoked for the common good and promulgated to the community by him who has the care of the community."[22] At the very outset, however, it must be stated that this definition is normally treated by commentators in relation to the written law. To be applicable to customary law it must undergo some adaptation. This thesis will be developed gradually.

The Angelic Doctor's definition of law contains three chief elements which apply with full force to customary law. Law is a regulation of right reason, invoked by authority for the common good.[23]

---

21. *De Legibus,* Lib. 7, c. 9, n. 10.

22. *Summa,* Ia IIae, q. 90, art. 4, *in corp.*

23. The writer proposes that there is no need to include the element of promulgation in the definition of customary law. The common usage of the people while inducing the future legal custom makes *ipso facto* for its promulgation.

As a *regulation* of right reason customary law must command or prohibit. Thus Suárez stated that the *mores* of the people take on the force of law when there is a sufficiency of acts which have to do with moral activity, as right or wrong, in relation to the common good. He added that just as it is of the essence of law that it command or prohibit, so the same requisite is postulated for customary law.[24]

Secondly, *authority* must be embodied in customary law. Here the difference between customary law and the written law is immediately evident. When a written law is published, it is the legislator who uses his authority to impose an obligation on those who are subject to his jurisdiction. But when customary law has been induced, it is the people who have determined the legitimate manner of acting.[25] The problem of this work is to discover *what people* may so determine the emergence of customary law. Saint Thomas, while discussing the authority attaching to law, defended the right of the people to act in this manner when he said:

> Ordinare autem aliquid in bonum est vel totius multitudinis vel alicuius gerentis vicem totius multitudinis.[26]

It is of particular importance to emphasize the rôle of the people as being that of the ones who induce an authoritative obligation in law when one defines the notion of law in its application to legal customs. The legislator acts impersonally, having supplied his contingent consent by way of anticipation in the written law. To insist upon the personal sanction of the legislator for the obligatory force of all law cannot but prejudice the student in his research regarding the possible capacity of lesser communities to induce customary law.

---

24. *De Legibus,* Lib. 7, c. 3, n. 6.

25. It is true that in the Church custom obtains the force of law *unice a consensu competentis Superioris ecclesiastici* (canon 25). However, it is the common opinion of the commentators that a *legal* consent of the competent ecclesiastical superior is sufficient, i. e., a custom of fact takes on the force of law *ipso facto* when there have been fulfilled the conditions which the written law enumerates as requisite for the achieving of this effect (cf. Van Hove, *De Consuetudine,* pp. 65-66). This fact supports the writer's contention that it is the people who determine the legitimate manner of acting in customary law.

26. *Summa,* Ia IIae, q. 90, art. 3, *in corp.*

Finally, law is directed to *the common good,* which is to say that law is directed to the good of a community. There are contained two notions in this clause. First is the notion of a community which has been defined as a plurality of persons distinguishable as a moral unit by reason of a common bond.[27] Second is the notion of the *good* of the community. Suárez defined this as its "peace and happiness,"[28] and it may be paraphrased as its right order and progress. Thus laws are directed to the right ordering of the external acts of the community and to the ensuring of the social progress of the persons morally united in the community. When a duly appointed superior makes a law, he must have in mind the good of the whole community subject to him. Similarly, when the people induce a custom, they must intend the good of the community, else their usage cannot eventuate as a just law. Perhaps it was in this light that Suárez defined law as a "common precept, which is just and stable in character."[29]

However, it is not the order and progress of any community whatsoever which is to be regulated by true law. Law looks primarily to the regulation of the "perfect" community, or that which has within it all the means necessary to conduct its members to the end proposed as necessary to them.[30] Saint Thomas expressed this truth in the following words:

> Primum autem principium in operativis . . . est finis ultimus. Est autem ultimus finis humanae vitae felicitas vel beatitudo. Unde oportet quod lex maxime respiciat ordinem qui est in beatitudine. Rursus cum omnis pars ordinetur ad totum, sicut imperfectum ad perfectum unus autem homo est pars communitatis perfectae, necesse est quod lex proprie respiciat ordinem ad felicitatem communem.[31]

---

27. Cf. *supra,* p. 69.

28. *De Legibus,* Lib. 1, c. 7, n. 4.

29. "Lex est commune praeceptum, justum ac stabile, sufficienter promulgatum." — *De Legibus,* Lib. 1, c. 12, n. 4. The writer omitted the note of promulgation from the definition as not being pertinent to customary law.

30. Cf. Cappello, *Summa Iuris Publici Ecclesiastici* (ed., altera Romae, 1928), n. 41.

31. *Summa,* Ia IIae, q. 90, art. 2, *in corp.*

Nevertheless, within the two "perfect" communities of the Church and the State[32] there are inferior communities whose common good is *de facto* regulated by law. Thus States are divided into cities and the universal Church is divided into dioceses. The common good of these communities is normally legislated for by the superiors at their head, though custom may serve as another mode of regulation. The most delicate problem of this dissertation will be to discover what inferior communities may be said to have a common good so related to the universal Church as to attach to them the capacity for being regulated by ecclesiastical law, so that in turn they may induce customary law.

ARTICLE 6. *The Notion of Ecclesiastical Law*

The one ecclesiastical polity under Christ is the Catholic Church, an altogether self-contained and autonomous society.[33] Since the Church is a society juridically complete in itself and independent of other societies, its competent ecclesiastical superiors have the right and the duty to make laws in so far as the ordering of the Church to its proper end, *viz.*, the sanctification and salvation of souls, demands this. Right order and progress within the Church may also be regulated by the people through their repeated acts which form customary ecclesiastical law. What groups of people are properly qualified so to induce legal customs will be discussed in the next two chapters.

---

32. Cf. Cappello, *op. cit.*, n. 43.

33. Leo XIII, ep. encycl. *Immortale Dei*, 1 Nov. 1885, n. 5: "Haec societas [Ecclesia], quamvis ex hominibus constet, non secus ac civilis communitas, tamen propter finem sibi constitutum, atque instrumenta, quibus ad finem contendit, supernaturalis est ac spiritualis: . . . et quod plurimum interest, societas est *genere et iure perfecta,* cum adiumenta ad incolumitatem actionemque suam necessaria, voluntate beneficioque Conditoris sui, omnia in se et per se ipso possideat." — *ASS,* XXVIII (1885), 752.

Chapter VII

THE COMMUNITY-SUBJECT OF A LEGISLATOR

The purpose of this chapter is to explain that in the Church any community which has a legislator at its immediate head is capable of inducing customary law. This chapter has the further purpose of defining the subjects who may so induce the law. It accordingly treats of these subjects collectively, as the total community, and distributively, as distinctive members of the community. Finally, relative to the common good it discusses the matter in which these subjects may induce legal customs.

The reason for delineating as able to induce customary law that community which has a legislator at its head derives from the use of the word *saltem* in canon 26, as discussed in the preceding chapter.[1] In treating of the force of this word, Van Hove (1872-1947) concluded that it is superfluous.[2] This view could well be defended if one were to argue that the word *saltem* as related to the phrase *communitas quae legis ecclesiasticae recipiendae capax est* bears simply the implication that those groups of persons who *make law* are *a fortiori* able to induce customary law. Such groups, however, are so few (being limited practically to the assemblies of bishops and to the chapter meetings held either by the major superiors of an exempt clerical institute or by the abbots of independent monasteries) as hardly to deserve mention. Therefore the writer is convinced that the word *saltem* has a historical significance of great value for determining the types of communities able to induce customary law.

The reader will recall that the phrase, *communitas cui lex imponi potest,* came into vogue only with the advent of Suárez as the determinant of the least "qualified community."[3] Before Suárez this qualified community was defined as *populus qui potest condere legem.* The

---

1. Cf. *supra,* p. 69.

2. Cf. *De Consuetudine,* p. 75.

3. Cf. *supra,* p. 40. The writer proposes henceforth to employ the phrase "qualified community" as an equivalent for "the community which has a capacity for inducing customary law." This selection seems warranted in view of the resulting simplified structure and expression.

statement implied in this definition was popularly received by commentators from the twelfth century onward in their desire to make it clear that all law, written or customary, took on its obligatory force from the consent of the legislator.[4] The phrase was not intended to convey the notion that only those groups of persons who were able to *make law* could also induce legal customs. Its purpose was to make clear the fact that for inducing legal customs the community had to act with the sanction of the legislator at its head. In this light one may say that there was never any dispute over the capacity to induce customary law on the part of that community at whose immediate head there was a legislator.

Of course, if the word *saltem* had not been included in canon 26, it would still be certain that the community which has a legislator at its immediate head is a qualified community for the inducing of customary law. Since such a community is *in fact* the subject of laws, it certainly has a *capacity* for receiving law. It is primarily the capacity of such communities that will be discussed in the following chapters, though some of the rules there to be considered will apply also to any communities which in this matter can be adjudged as qualified.

ARTICLE 1. *Legislators in the Church*

The supreme legislator over the Church is the Roman Pontiff, the Vicar of Christ.[5] He rules with ordinary power over that majestic community which is the Church. Though the Church is not regularly referred to as a community, it is vested with all the elements necessary to qualify as a community. The Church is a universal group of persons, united under the Supreme Pontiff in the bonds of a common faith, in the observance of a common discipline and in the use of a common sacramental system. Universal customary law has been and may still be induced in the Church.

Our Blessed Lord did not intend that the Supreme Pontiff should ensure the common good of the Church in all its parts through the use of his legislative power alone. By divine constitution the Supreme Pontiff is assisted in the government of the Church by subordinate

4. Cf. *supra*, p. 16.
5. Cf. canon 218.

rulers, namely by the bishops who as the successors of the Apostles are also vested with ordinary power to legislate.[6] Thus, while each bishop must legislate in view of the common good of the whole Church (according to the norms of the sacred canons),[7] yet he may establish particular statutes, law in the full sense of the term, to maintain good order within his diocese and to particularize the universal law according to the needs of his subjects.[8]

Each diocese is a true community of persons united under the local ordinary in accord with the constitution of the Church. Each diocese may be considered as having a common good within itself, subject to regulation. Further, this regulation is normally obtained through episcopal statutes, which are true law. The reason why episcopal statutes have the force of true law is that the common good of each diocese is integrally related to the common good of the universal Church and ensures the well-being of the whole Church.

This is an important concept for the understanding of the next chapter of this study. While any fixed and permanent group of persons may be said to have a common good which demands regulation, it does not follow that all are to be regulated by law. Law is primarily directed to the common good of the members of a completely self-contained society,[9] and accordingly regulation by law applies primarily to those fixed and permanent groups which contribute in a notable measure to

---

6. Leo XIII, ep. encycl. *Satis cognitum,* 29 iun. 1896, n. 25: "Quo modo Petri auctoritatem in Romano Pontifice perpetuam permanere necesse est, sic Episcopi, qui succedunt Apostolis, horum potestatem ordinariam hereditate capiunt, ita ut intimam Ecclesiae constitutionem ordo Episcoporum necessario attingat. Quamquam vero neque plenam neque universalem ii, neque summam obtinent auctoritatem, non tamen *vicarii* Romanorum Pontificum putandi, quia potestatem gerunt sibi propriam, verissimeque popularum quas regunt, antistites *ordinarii* dicuntur." *ASS,* XXVIII (1896), 732.

7. Cf. canon 335, § 1.—"Ius ipsis et officium est gubernandi dioecesim tum in spiritualibus tum in temporalibus cum potestate legislativa, iudiciaria, coactiva ad normam sacrorum canonum exercenda."

8. Other territorial divisions of the universal Church at whose head is a legislator are apostolic vicariates and prefectures, abbacies and prelacies *nullius.* These will be discussed in particular in Chapter IX.

9. Cf. *supra,* p. 72, in which a key phrase of the writings of Saint Thomas, "necesse est quod lex proprie respiciat ordinem ad felicitatem communem," is explained.

the order and progress of that society. In the case of a diocese its adequate relation to the well-being of the universal Church has been defined in the constitution of the Church whereby resident bishops are vested with ordinary power to legislate.

Certain religious superiors and the chapters of exempt clerics also have legislative jurisdiction over the members of the community in virtue of canon 501, § 1.[10] Therefore, whenever such legislative power is present in a community, its common good is consequently subject to regulation by true law, and the community must be adjudged qualified for the inducing of customary law.

ARTICLE 2. *The Subject of Law Collectively*

In defining the capacity for inducing customary law, which capacity attaches to those communities at whose immediate head there is a legislator, one must discuss in some detail what persons can compose such communities. Canon 12 states in a negative form who is to be considered as a proper subject of ecclesiastical law: not subject to that law are all those persons who have not been baptized, the baptized who do not enjoy a sufficient use of reason and also the baptized who, though they have acquired the use of reason, are not at least seven years of age, as long as the law has not made contrary provisions.[11] All those persons, then, who do not fall within any of the three mentioned categories are subjects of the ecclesiastical law. And as groups it is only those persons who are in communion with the Church that can be considered the subject of law.[12]

The question now arises: How many such persons within a legislative jurisdiction must execute repeated acts in order to induce a cus-

10. Superiores et Capitula . . . in religione clericali autem exempta habent iurisdictionem ecclesiasticam tam pro foro interno quam pro externo.

11. "Legibus mere ecclesiasticis non tenentur qui baptismum non receperunt, nec baptizati qui sufficienti rationis usu non gaudent, nec qui, licet rationis usum assecuti, septimum aetatis annum nondum expleverunt, nisi aliud iure expresse caveatur."

12. To what extent infidels, heretics and schismatics as individuals are the subjects of ecclesiastical law is a much discussed question. The discussion of course adverts to such persons *as individuals.* As groups they are not to be considered as subjects of law, since they contribute nothing to the good order and progress of the Church (cf. *infra,* p. 116).

tomary law that becomes binding upon all the potential subjects within the jurisdiction? The answer is to be sought in the similarity that exists between the written law of the legislator and the customary law of the community, since the written and the customary law are both of the same nature.

It is for the good of the whole community that the legislator must establish his written laws. Suárez, commenting on the words of Saint Isidore of Seville (+636), namely that laws must be established for the common good and not for anyone's private benefit, said:

> ... non de communitate cui imponenda sit lex loquitur, sed solum docet *pro utilitate communi* imponendam esse, cuicumque imponatur.[13]

Giving further evidence that all jurists agreed that law of its nature must be directed to the common good, he quoted Plato (+347 B. C.):

> Conditur, mea quidem sententia, utilitatis gratia lex, et ad maximum civitatis bonum legem concedunt legislatores, legeque sublata, legitime in civitate vivere non possumus.[14]

Similarly, when a community elects to bind itself to customary law, it is necessary that the common good of the whole community be protected. Only the repeated acts of the whole community can supply sufficient evidence that the customary law as induced is for the good of the community. Thus, a single individual who acted in a private capacity would appear ridiculous if he alleged that he had induced a customary law for a community through his own private acts. In like fashion a minority of the community would act without warrant in seeking to induce a legal custom for the whole community. However, if the major part of the community has acted, then that action must be considered as standing for the action of the whole community. This is a dictate of reason which was stressed in the Roman Law when it stated: "Refertur ad universos, quod publice fit per maiorem partem."[15] Therefore, to induce a customary law which within a qualified community, can be-

---

13. *De Legibus,* Lib. I, c. 6, n. 4 (italics furnished by the writer).
14. *Ibid.,* c. 7, n. 2.
15. D. (50, 17) 160.

come binding on the whole community, at least the major portion of the community which in its members does not fall within any of the three categories enumerated in canon 12 must have given its consent through the repeated acts performed by it.

ARTICLE 3. *The Subject of Law Distributively*

Every just law must be directed to the common good of the whole community for which it is made. But it does not follow that every law will apply with equal force to each member of the community. Saint Paul implied this when he said:

> For just as in one body we have many members, yet all the members have not the same function, so we, the many, are one body in Christ, but severally members one of another. But we have gifts differing according to the grace that has been given us, such as prophecy . . .; or ministry . . .; or he who teaches . . .; he who exhorts . . .; he who gives . . .; he who presides . . .; he who shows mercy. . . .[16]

While there must be ecclesiastical laws to regulate each of the activities mentioned by Saint Paul, each body of laws will apply directly only to those in turn who prophesy, who minister, who teach, etc.

Michiels (writing of laws which proceed immediately from a legislator) well expresses this distributive aspect in laws. He states that it is indeed required, but that it also suffices in a law that it apply in general to the physical persons making up the community, i. e., that it pertain to each and every member of the community as a member of the community and *according to the exigency of the matter.*[17] In explaining the phrase, "according to the exigency of the matter," Michiels states that the lawmaker need not pass each law for the right regulation of the sum total of the members of the community, regarded collectively, but he may view the community *distributively,* and legislate directly for

16. Rom. XII: 4-8. The version used by the writer is that edited by the Confraternity of Christian Doctrine (Paterson, N. J.: St. Anthony Guild Press, 1941).

17. *Normae Generales,* I, 139.

certain distinct members in view of their common duty, office, condition, quality or locale.[18]

Suárez proposed the same thought in his treatise on law. He taught that it was possible for a law to be passed simply for a particular category of persons in a community, and not for the rest, in view of a certain public duty or office common to certain members, in consideration of a common condition or state of life, or in consequence of a certain locale or territory in which some of the members of the community lived.[19] He qualified the last-mentioned aspect of the distributive character in a community, namely when the element of territory figured as the determining factor, in the following words: "... ita ut non tantum pro his qui nunc habitant, sed durabiliter per successionem indifferenter [lex] feratur."[20] In the same passage he further delineated the element of territory as that which may lend a distinctive aspect to its inhabitants. He stated that the legislator may judge that the community has need of a particular service of the persons living in a special territory, or that the condition of the persons in that territory may be such as to require a particular law.[21]

In summary, then, one may conclude that a distinctive group of persons within a qualified community may be considered the proper subject of ecclesiastical law on either one of two grounds: 1) in consideration of their public duty or office, and 2) in view of their particular state of life. Suárez himself reduced the division of distinctive groups within a community to these two in a passage wherein he stated:

> ... leges impositae sunt, obligantes haec vel illa membra, juxta eorum munera et capacitatem.[22]

Therefore persons distributed within a qualified community can be considered the proper subject of law in view of their common state of life or in view of their common activity relating to the good of the

18. *Loc. cit.*
19. *De Legibus,* Lib. I, c. 6, n. 24.
20. *Loc. cit.*
21. *Loc. cit.*
22. *Ibid.,* n. 9.

community. There are numerous states of life: childhood, adulthood, the clerical state, the religious state, the lay state, etc. Similarly, there are numerous activities of importance to the communal good: there are legislators, judges, pastors, parents, etc.

Now, even as laws may be written for a distinctive class of persons distributed in a qualified community, so may these persons (who alone are qualified to act in the particular circumstances) induce a customary law, which while contributing to the good of the whole community is directed primarily to them in view of their office or state of life.

ARTICLE 4. *The Acts of the Community Which Are Related to the Common Good*

It has been repeatedly stated in this study that all law must look to the good of the community to which it is directed. It must bind all the members of the community, or at least those who are made subject to its command. Likewise, the *object* of the law, or the matter being regulated, must have a bearing on the common good of the community. In civil societies the matter of the common good is more easily ascertained than in the Church. For in civil societies law normally regulates the interactivities of the members, whereby social justice is to be attained. But in the communities of the Church the sanctification of all the members is the *finis proprius,* and not only in so far as this is common to all the members, but also in so far as it is proper to *each single member.*[23]

While it is not within the scope of this dissertation to discuss the object of customary law, it is important for the reader to keep in mind that no community of persons may induce a legal custom through private activities or through such as have no relation to the common good of ecclesiastical societies. The acts may not be altogether private, for the common consent and the concerted activity of the community which induces a legal custom are essential features.[24] That the acts must also

23. Cf. Michiels, *Normae Generales,* I, 143.

24. Cf. Suárez: "... id quod maxime est substantiale et essentiale consuetudini, scil., ut sit communi populi consensu recepta." — *De Legibus,* Lib. 7, c. 2, n. 1.

redound to the good order and progress of the community in the achieving of its proper end is evident.[25]

At this point it may be said with certainty that those communities which have a legislator at their immediate head are able to induce a customary law. The qualified members of such communities, viewed collectively or distributively, have this capacity in any matter that lends itself as fitted for this purpose. All the authors whom the writer was able to consult agree in this. Van Hove confirms the fact that it is the common opinion.[26]

But before introducing the next chapter one may point to certain authors who either expressly or in their examples deny that any lesser community can be considered as a qualified community. Among these are Berutti, apprehensive lest too great a multitude of particular customs arise;[27] Cocchi, who in harking back to the *perfecta communitas* of Suárez interprets it with exclusive reference to communities in which there is legislative power;[28] Augustine (+1943), who averred that lesser communities lack what he called the "necessary autonomy;"[29] Coronata, who prefers to suspend judgment with reference to the lesser communities;[30] and Falco (+1943), who read into canon 26 a distinction between *customs* induced by collective groups which are amenable to ecclesiastical authority and *observances* practiced by the lesser collegiate bodies.[31]

---

25. For a study of the rational aspects demanded in valid customary law, and for an explanation of the *animus se obligandi* as postulated for the qualified community which establishes a factual custom *praeter legem,* the reader may refer to any of the post-Code authors listed in the bibliography appended to this work, all of whom discuss the whole tract of custom.

26. *De Consuetudine,* p. 76.

27. *Institutiones Iuris Canonici* (6 vols., Vol. I, Taurini-Romae: Marietti, 1936), I, 100-101 (hereafter cited *Institutiones*).

28. *Commentarium in Codicem Iuris Canonici* (8 vols. in 5, Vol. I. 5. ed., Taurinorum Augustae: Marietti, 1938), I, 218 (hereafter cited *Commentarium*). In agreement with Cocchi is Sipos, *Enchiridion Iuris Canonici* (Pécs: ex Typographis "Haladas R. T.," 1926), p. 52.

29. *A Commentary on the New Code of Canon Law* (8 vols., Vol. I, 3. ed., St. Louis, Mo.: B. Herder Co., 1920), I, 109.

30. *Institutiones Iuris Canonici* (ed. altera, 5 vols., Vol. I, Taurini: Marietti, 1939), I, 41.

31. *Introduzione allo Studio del "Codex Iuris Canonici"* (Torino: Fratelli Bocca, 1925), pp. 120-122.

CHAPTER VIII

LESSER COMMUNITIES WITH A CAPACITY FOR INDUCING CUSTOMARY LAW

This chapter is devoted to ascertaining whether there may be communities which without a legislator at their immediate head can nevertheless have a capacity for inducing customary law. Judgment will be founded according to canon 26 on the presence in such communities of the capacity for receiving ecclesiastical law. The chapter is divided into three articles. First there is offered a general defense for the possible existence of such communities. Secondly there is presented a principle in the light of which one can determine for which of the lesser communities one may still acknowledge the capacity for inducing a customary law. Finally there are summarized the theories of the various authors.

ARTICLE 1. *A General Defense*

In the law there are numerous indications which give assurance that some communities without a legislator at their immediate head have nevertheless a capacity for inducing customary law. The word *saltem,* as seen in its historical background, bears the connotation that those communities which are amenable to an immediate legislative authority are certainly qualified in this matter, and that lesser communities may possess the same qualification.[1] Further evidence for this is found in the significant change in the wording of canon 26 when the new Code was being compiled. In the *Schema* of the Code, edited by Cardinal Gasparri, the wording of canon 26 was this:

> Communitas quae propriis legibus non regitur, nequit consuetudinem inducere quae vim legis obtineat.[2]

The wording, "communitas quae propriis legibus non regitur," is found in equivalent phrases in the writings of Suárez in such examples

1. Cf. *supra,* p. 69.

2. *Schema Codicis Iuris Canonici Pii Papae X,* cum notis Petri Card. Gasparri (2 vols., Vol. I, Romae, 1912), Lib. I, canon 26.

as "communitates perfectae, seu civitates aut populi, qui possunt propriis legibus communibus obligari,"[3] and again, "communitas quae sit capax potestatis legislativae pro seipsa."[4] These phrases were used by Suárez in designation of the "capacity" of communities in which there obtained an *active* legislative power. Then, in his delineation of the least of the qualified communities, or the one in which there obtained at least a *passive* legislative power,[5] he used the phrases, "saltem sufficiens ut vera lex illi imponi potest,"[6] and again, ". . . non potest ius spiritualis consuetudinis (ut sic dicam) introduci nisi in subjecto capaci legis ecclesiastici."[7]

Though the reader must be cautioned in regard to the intermingling of civil and canonical legal theory in these passages of Suárez, and against drawing too sweeping a conclusion from them (for Suárez did not write law, he simply proposed theories), yet one is inclined to believe that in the final presentation of canon 26 the most liberal wording of Suárez was employed.

Again, in the history of the canon law that relates to the inducing of legal customs there are repeated instances in which cities and "particular localities" were acknowledged as having induced customary law. The reader may refer in particular to Article 3 of Chapter V of this work for confirmation of this fact. In the Code itself "local customs" are to be followed in the regulation of the place of burial,[8] of the amount of the funeral stipend,[9] of the law with regard to fasting,[10] of the holding of processions in churches,[11] of the tenure of certain rights of families which enjoy the *ius patronatus* in a church,[12] and of the payment of tithes and first fruits.[13] Though in the Code there is no

3. *De Legibus,* Lib. 7, c. 3, n. 10.
4. *Ibid.,* c. 9, n. 6.
5. For Suárez' distinction between active and passive legislative power in a community, cf. *supra,* pp. 40-41.
6. *Loc. cit.*
7. *De Legibus,* Lib. 7, c. 9, n. 10.
8. Canon 1230, § 1.
9. Canon 1234, § 1.
10. Canon 1251, § 1.
11. Canon 1291, § 1 and canon 1294, § 1.
12. Canon 1455, 3°.
13. Canon 1502.

specification of the extent of the territory in which these particular and local customs must have been induced, yet the matters there mentioned leave room for the interpretation that the region may well be of less extension than a whole diocese.

Another indication in the Code that the qualified community may be such in character that it is without a legislator at its immediate head is found in canon 63, § 1. In this canon it is stated that privileges may be acquired through legitimate custom.[14] Therefore, while the requirements of the duration of time and of reasonableness in the character of the usage, as also the demand of a legal capacity in the community must all be verified for the inducing of a legal custom, the produced effect may be that of the gaining of a privilege. Now, a privilege is a private law, which confers some special and permanent benefit or favor, either as something to which the law itself is opposed or to which it does not advert.[15] When a privilege is accorded to a group, it is not necessarily all the members of a complete legislative jurisdiction whose good is sought, though the whole community may be benefited.[16] Herein, again, is an indication in the Code that one may sustain a liberal view regarding what lesser community may still be regarded as a qualified community.

While none of the alleged indications which point to the tenableness of a broad interpretation of canon 26 is individually conclusive in its force, yet in combination they do incline the student toward a serious investigation of the possible existence of qualified communities even when they do not have a legislator at their immediate head.

ARTICLE 2. *A Principle for the Determination of Capacity in a Community*

The precise question of this article seems accurately phrased by Michiels when he asks what communities, *as single bodies,* have a ca-

14. Canon 63, § 1.—"Privilegia acquiri possunt non solum per directam concessionem competentis auctoritatis et per communicationem, sed etiam per legitimam consuetudinem aut praescriptionem."

15. Cf. Beste, *Introductio in Codicem* (3. ed., Collegeville, Minn.: St. John's Abbey Press, 1946), p. 119.

16. Cf. Beste, *loc. cit.*

pacity for receiving true law.[17] In answering this question the commentators cover a wide range of opinions, particularly in their enumeration of the various communities of this kind. On the one extreme there are those who have been cited in the final paragraph of the preceding chapter,[18] who beyond all question accept as qualified communities only those bodies in which there is an intrinsic legislative power. On the other extreme one may cite Ojetti (1862-1932), who wrote:

> Imo si loquamur . . . per se et ex natura rei, . . . puto omnem communitatem, quaecumque illa sit, etsi sit simplex familia, posse per se dispositive inducere consuetudinem. . . .[19]

To arrive at some principle by which to determine the capacity of a community for receiving law one may examine the nature of certain "imperfect communities" which are *in fact* regulated by law.[20] These communities lend themselves to this examination for though they are not autonomous or independent, they do have legislation proper to themselves. A diocese is an example of such an ecclesiastical community, a city of a civic community. The constitutive notes of such a community are these: it is composed of 1) a group of persons, 2) morally united (normally territorially, but not necessarily, e. g., not in the case of exempt religious), 3) pursuing a common end (civil or ecclesiastical) by common activities, and 4) subject in these activities to regulations binding under the authority of a legislator. The first three notes of such a community are common to the very notion of any community. But the fourth note is distinctive of a community which is *in fact* regulated by law.

For what reason, then, are legislators put at the head of these imperfect communities? Why are cities chartered by a state, and why are particular dioceses established? The answer seems to be that *the common good* of these *communities within themselves is sufficiently related*

---

17. Cf. *Normae Generales,* I, 140.

18. Cf. *supra,* p. 82.

19. Ojetti, *Commentarium in Codicem Iuris Canonici* (4 vols., Vol. I, Romae: Apud Aedes Universitatis Gregorianae, 1927), I, 175.

20. The writer employs the term "imperfect community" here in the sense that the communities used as examples are not strictly perfect in that they have not within themselves all the means necessary to attain their proper end.

to the good of the perfect society of which they are a part to call for their subjection to regulations which may have the binding force of true law.

Now, canon 26 does not demand that the qualified community be *in fact* regulated by its own laws. It simply demands that the community have a *capacity* for receiving ecclesiastical law. Therefore that community may be considered to have a capacity for receiving ecclesiastical law when *its common good is sufficiently related to the good of the Church to permit its activities to be regulated by law.*

Arguing from this premise the writer proposes that such is the case whenever a community of persons *is canonically approved by competent ecclesiastical authority.* Canonical approval is that positive approval of a community which in accordance with law is expressed through a canonical erection, through canonical recognition, through the granting of particular statutes, or through the sanctioning of a constitution. It is not to be identified with the mere commendation of a group nor with the blessing of a project by an ecclesiastical dignitary. Canonical approval is to be understood as a thing that can be granted only by those who are ordinaries according to the delineation contained in canon 198, § 1.[21]

This canonical approval gives evidence that the approved community has been incorporated into the structure of the Church. By this approval the community is vested with juridic status. The activities of its members are judged by competent ecclesiastical authority as worthy of recognition in law. Thus the good which an approved community pursues through its common activities must be judged sufficiently related to the common good of the Church to permit of its regulation by law. In the examination of particular communities in the following chapters the various modes of canonical approval will be exemplified and thus clarified. It suffices here to state and demonstrate the principle.

---

21. "In iure nomine Ordinarii intelliguntur, nisi quis expresse excipiatur, praeter Romanum Pontificem, pro suo quisque territorio Episcopus residentialis, Abbas vel Praelatus *nullius* eorumque Vicarius Generalis, Administrator, Vicarius et Praefectus Apostolicus, itemque iis qui praedictis deficientibus interim ex iuris praescripto aut ex probatis constitutionibus succedunt in regimine, pro suis vero subditis Superiores maiores in religionibus clericalibus exemptis."

While it is true that on only rare occasions would a legislator impose a law exclusively on one community within his jurisdiction, yet one must reflect that customary law arises from the concerted acts of a "people" (*populus*), and nothing more than the *legal* sanction of competent ecclesiastical authority is required. In such an event it is the community that through a factual custom at least *determines* the legal obligation which later can become binding for it.

If one adverts to the definition of law as proposed by Suárez, a "common precept, which is just and stable,"[22] one may more readily consent to the possible inducing of a customary law by a community which is without a legislator at its immediate head. The legal custom will be *common* for the reason that it was induced through the usage of the whole community. The *just* aspect of the legal custom is sufficiently provided for in the fulfillment of the conditions which the written law demands for its reasonableness.[23] Its *stability* is assured through the fact that according to the demand of the law its usage has continued for the requisite duration of time.[24] And the *preceptive force* attaching to true law is sufficiently safeguarded through the fact that the qualified community has a juridic status, is incorporated into the structure of the Church, and is pursuing a good recognized as important to the common good of the Church, all of which factors derive from the canonically given approval for the existence of the community.

ARTICLE 3. *Other Theories on the Least of the Qualified Communities*

Post-Code commentators almost without exception cite Suárez in defense of their views on the qualified community. The very diversity of the conclusions at which they arrive gives evidence that Suárez did not resolve the problem in any definitive manner. Certain authors retain the exact wording of Suárez and accept his doctrine as satisfactorily ex-

---

22. Cf. *De Legibus,* Lib. I, c. 12, n. 4. Cf. also *supra,* pp. 70-73, for the adaptation of the notion of law to customary law.

23. Cf. canon 27.

24. Cf. canon 27.

plaining the law of the Code. Cappello's procedure is a case in point. The key passage in his presentation is this:

> The subject capable of inducing a legal custom is each and every community which is at least relatively perfect, i. e., "which is at least capable of receiving ecclesiastical law." And for the concept of a community relatively perfect there is required a certain autonomy, or a proper rule and a distinctive unity (*proprium regimen et peculiaris unitas*).[25]

Now, any community, i. e., any group of persons morally united by reason of a common bond, is *unified* in its very definition and must have a body of regulations, or a *proper rule,* if it is to remain a unified community and seek the end for which it is morally bound together. The precise question then is, "When do the regulations by which a community is governed take on the force of law?" If one seeks to find the answer in the writings of Suárez, one may contend that it is when a community is integrated into the structure of a "perfect" society, so that it is not either without a governing head or devoid of all related co-operation with competent ecclesiastical authority under the latter's control.[26] While by some this view may be considered a far-fetched interpretation of Suárez, yet it has the advantage of being concise and clear, and, what is more important, it has also its own intrinsic merit.

Stability in a community as bound together under some head is the factor which, as Vermeersch-Creusen contend, determines the capacity of the community for receiving law. This thesis is contained in the following passage:

> A community is a group of persons bound together for some end and under some head. But such a community will not have the capacity for receiving law (which the Code expressly demands)

---

25. Cappello, *Summa Iuris Canonici* (3 vols., Vol. I, 4 ed., Romae: apud sedes Universitatis Gregorianae, 1945), I, pp. 88-89. Also founding their argument in the *perfecta communitas* of Suárez are Wernz-Vidal, *Ius Canonicum* (7 vols. in 8, Romae: Apud Aedes Universitatis Gregorianae, Vol. I, 1938; Vol. II, 3. ed., a P. Philippo Aguirre recognita, 1943; Vol. IV, Pars I, 1934; Vol. IV, Pars II, 1935), I, n. 236.

26. Cf. *supra,* p. 41.

unless it be stable, or *per se perpetua.* For law is by definition perpetual.[27]

The vagueness of this thesis makes it difficult to analyze and judge. How stable must the community be? Must it be stable in the sense that it is a necessary community? Is not the bond of union of the community of any importance? Is it to be assumed that the community bears some relation to order and progress in the Church? Since all law must be directed to the common good and primarily to the good of a perfect society, is the stability of a community sufficient evidence of its relation to the common good, and specifically to the good of the Church?

The choice of the sole note of stability as the determining factor of the qualified community can lead to much misunderstanding. The fact of the matter is that any qualified community must engage in a factual custom through forty years at least before the practice will take on the force of law. After that the induced customary law retains its legal value only while the community remains of the same nature. Therefore the stability which must be present in law is sufficiently guaranteed in the temporal conditions which are postulated for the inducing of customary law. Beyond that the stability attendant upon law varies with the kind of law that is established. The moral law expressed in the canons of the Code is altogether stable, for the doing of good and the shunning of evil always exist as commands of the law.[28] But disciplinary laws, by which the social order in particular is preserved and maintained, opportunely direct the members of the society *in accord with the variety of times and conditions.*[29] The very notion of the existence of legal customs which stand in opposition to statute law must suppose that the law be not so stable that it cannot yield to alteration.

27. Vermeersch-Creusen, *Epitome Iuris Canonici,* II, pp. 130-131. Special emphasis is also placed upon the note of stability in the community by Cicognani, *Canon Law* (Authorized English Version by J. M. O'Hara and F. Brennan, 2. ed., Philadelphia: Dolphin Press, 1935; Reprint: Westminster, Md.: The Newman Bookshop, 1947), pp. 647-648.

28. Cf. Cappello, *Summa Iuris Publici Ecclesiastici,* n. 171.

29. *Ibid.,* n. 168.

In the end, the note of stability in law seems sufficiently protected when the qualified community is made determinable as such through the canonical approval of competent ecclesiastical authority for its very existence. Through that approval the community becomes incorporated into the structure of the Church, being by that act regarded as a permanent adjunct of the Church.

Other commentators propose the theory that a community may be adjudged as qualified when it has at its head a superior with a public office (*munus publicum*), for then the community can be regarded as established for the common good. Van Hove presented this theory in the following passage:

> To solve the controversy in respect to other communities one must look to the very nature of law, whose essential element is not perpetuity, but a regulation for the common good. Therefore a group is capable of receiving law when at its head there is a superior who holds a public office, i. e., an office established for the common good.[30]

Again, it is extremely difficult to decipher the principle contained in this passage for want of any explanation of what a *munus publicum* is. It is only certain that Van Hove did not regard the *munus publicum* as an office to which legislative power is necessarily attached, for he agreed that there is no dispute about the capacity of communities which are regulated by one who holds such power. It is useless, though, to attempt to read into the principle a meaning in accord with the theory the writer has proposed. Such a conclusion could not in fairness be attributed to Van Hove. But there is agreement on the fact that the qualified community must bear a relation to the common good demanded in law.

Moral personality is made the determining factor of the qualified community by Couly, a French canonist. His statement to this effect follows:

30. *De Consuetudine,* p. 77. Also of this opinion are Beste (*Introductio in Codicem,* p. 95) and Guilfoyle (*Custom,* The Catholic University of America Canon Law Studies, n. 105 [Washington, D. C.: The Catholic University of America, 1937], pp. 93-96).

> The idea of custom supposes necessarily the idea of a collectivity, and only those collectivities which have an existence in fact and in law so that they are constituted as moral persons, can give rise to custom. But the numerical extension of the community bears little weight. It is not necessary that the collectivity enjoy legislative power or even dominative power of ruling; it suffices that it be such as to be the proper subject of laws.[31]

The writer agrees that moral persons in the Church do constitute qualified communities, but in the subsequent discussion of particular communities it will be shown that other collectivities or aggregations which are minus the status of moral persons can likewise be regarded as qualified communities. For example, canonical approbation can be given to an association of persons even though it is not established simultaneously as a moral personality. Moreover, it is not strictly the *moral personality* of a community of persons which gives it a capacity for inducing customary law. For moral personality can attach to a non-collegiate as well as to a collegiate body or institute, either of which thus acquires the status of a natural person before the law.[32] So it appears unwarranted and inadmissible to regard all juridical moral personalities in the Church as the equivalent of communities capable of being made the subjects of ecclesiastical law. The community which is contemplated in canon 26 is any group of persons which is morally united by a common bond, but which exists with each person retaining his individuality.[33] The *capacity* for inducing a legal custom derives from the fact that canonical approbation has been accorded to the collectivity, regardless of whether it is erected as a moral person.

Finally, there are those authors who in determining the capacity of a community for inducing legal customs require all the notes that essentially relate to written law itself. They demand stability, a communal aspect, and a juridic status, before a community can be regarded as

---

31. A. Couly, "La Coutume en Droit Canonique," *Le Canoniste,* XLVIII (1926), 428-441.

32. Cf. *supra,* p. 67.

33. Cf. *supra,* p. 68.

qualified for the inducing of customary law.[34] The writer feels that he has sufficiently demonstrated that the notes of stability and of a communal aspect attach to all such ecclesiastical communities which have received canonical approbation from a competent ecclesiastical superior.

It now remains only to appraise the status of the individual communities in the Church, and in the discussion to exemplify and clarify the relevant note of canonical approbation, by which ultimately the capacity of a community for inducing customary law appears to be determined and established.

---

34. Among these are Michiels (*Normae Generales,* I, 141-142), Toso (*Commentaria Minora,* I, 77-78), Kinane ("The Community Capable of Introducing Custom," *The Irish Ecclesiastical Record,* 5. series, XXXVIII [1931], 523-524), and Regatillo (*Institutiones Iuris Canonici* [2. ed., 2 vols., Vol. I, Sal Terrae: Santander, 1946], I, 80). Regatillo is noteworthy in his comprehensive list of possibilities of qualified communities.

PART III

THE COMMUNITIES IN PARTICULAR ABLE TO INDUCE LEGAL CUSTOMS

INTRODUCTION

The notion of "community" which has been arrived at from a study of the word itself and from its use in the Code is this: a plurality of persons, readily distinguishable as a unit by reason of a common bond, within which nonetheless each member of the community retains his individuality and is responsible for his individual actions.[1] Therefore, each group of persons to be examined herein must meet this definition of a community. However, it must be borne in mind that the established customary law may rest upon a community as a collective unit, i. e., upon the sum-total of the members of the community so that each one of the community is subject to the law directly, or the induced customary law may rest upon a community in a distributive sense, i. e., simply upon certain persons within the community so that they alone are the direct subjects of the law in consequence of some distinctive condition or of a particular state of life. In studying certain particular communities, then, the possibility of the existence of distinctive groups within that community will be considered. And as often as there is legislative power within the community, the latter's ability to induce customary law may be considered certain. The ability of lesser communities must be classified as at least probable in view of the opinion which with considerable warrant regards them as properly qualified communities for the inducing of customary law.

A fourfold division will comprise the chief communities within the framework of the Church. These are:

1) Communities of *territorial* extension, viz., the universal Church, a nation (or the ambit of a plenary Council), a province, a diocese (and its equivalents: the *abbatia nullius*, the *praelatura nullius*, the *praefectura apostolica*, and the *vicariatus apostolicus*), the deanery (or

---

1. Cf. *supra*, p. 66.

foraneus vicariatus), and the parish (with its equivalents: the quasi-parish, the national parish, and the personal parish).

2) Communities of religious, the divisions of which will be treated under a special title.

3) Associations of the laity, chief among which are archconfraternities, confraternities, primary unions, pious unions, third orders secular, and certain other associations of the laity which have received only the commendation of Church authority.

4) Institutes canonically erected for charitable, religious, or educational purposes.

CHAPTER IX

COMMUNITIES TERRITORIALLY EXTENDED

All commentators are in accord on the fact that those communities within which there is operative a true legislative power have a capacity for inducing legal custom. This is evident by implication from the word *saltem* in canon 26. If the community which has a capacity "at least for receiving ecclesiastical law" can induce a legal custom, then *a fortiori* the community in which there is operative an authority constituted for the making of ecclesiastical law can certainly induce legal custom. Therefore all territorially extended communities in the Church from the diocese and its equivalents on, through the various groupings of dioceses, to the universal Church can certainly induce legal customs. Only brief space, then, need be given to an examination of each of these types of community.

ARTICLE 1. *The Universal Church*

That the universal Catholic Church is a juridically perfect society is a first principle of public ecclesiastical law. And being a society which is juridically perfect, the Church has the full and inviolable right to make laws for the good order of Christian society. Therefore, since legislative power is operative in the universal Church, the universal community of Catholics, as subject to this power, may in virtue of canon 26 induce a legal custom. Furthermore, great segments within the universal Church which are distinct by reason of peculiarly applicable conditions (e. g., the persons in missionary lands, or Orientals) or by reason of the particular state of life (e. g., the laity, clerics, or bishops) may likewise induce a legal custom in view of their proper subjection to the universal law.

Though today this capacity in the universal Church does not present itself very forcefully, yet in the formation of the common law it was a very powerful and active factor. Chelodi (1880-1922) expressed this truth concisely in the following passage:

> Consuetudinem magnas partes habuisse in efformanda Ecclesiae disciplina notum est. Plura iuridica instituta (ex. gr. coelibatus, im-

pedimenta matrimonialia, ius patronatus) quae hucusque durant ac procedente tempore etiam legibus ordinata sunt, ab initio moribus populi sunt introducta.[2]

ARTICLE 2. *Territories within the Ambit of Plenary and Provincial Councils*

It would have been altogether legitimate in this title to have discussed nations and (in the light of the conditions in this country) federated states as communities able to induce a legal custom rather than the territorial ambit of plenary and provincial councils. Either of these divisions of territory could have been regarded as next in extension to the universal Church. But it seems preferable to remain within the framework of true ecclesiastical communities in the discussion of those groups of persons which have a capacity for receiving ecclesiastical law.

The ambit of jurisdiction of a provincial council is that territory which comprises a number of dioceses which by way of confederation have been legitimately erected as an ecclesiastical province by the authority of the Holy See.[3] And the ambit of jurisdiction of a plenary council comprises the territory of as many ordinaries as are assembled in it from a group of adjoining provinces, again under the authorization of the Holy See.[4]

The Catholics subject to either of these jurisdictions can certainly induce legal customs, since they are ecclesiastical communities in which there is operative a true legislative power. Again, the bishops of an ecclesiastical province or of the several provinces which come within the ambit of a plenary council can themselves by frequent and concerted acts induce legal customs, since they constitute a true community (or a plurality of persons united in the common bond of their episcopal character) and have the capacity not merely to receive but also to make ecclesiastical law.

---

2. *Ius Canonicum de Personis* (3. ed. curavit P. Ciprotti, Vicenza: Società Anonima Tipografica, 1942), p. 119.

3. Canon 215, § 1.

4. Canon 281.

ARTICLE 3. *The Diocese and Other Jurisdictions Similar to It*

The diocese, the prefecture apostolic, the vicariate apostolic, the abbacy *nullius*, and the prelacy *nullius* are the last of the territorially extended communities in which there is operative a true legislative power; thus each of these communities may induce legal customs. The residential bishop, the prefect apostolic, the vicar apostolic, the abbot *nullius* and the prelate *nullius*, the rulers respectively of these various communities, all enjoy ordinary power to legislate.[5] Evidently, if their subjects were unable to receive ecclesiastical law, their legislative power would be a mere figment.

Furthermore, within each of these communities there exist groups of persons truly distinct by reason of their proper state of life or in consequence of the divergent particular conditions which obtain. Since these groups are capable of receiving true law for the common good of the complete jurisdiction, they may also induce legal customs. Examples of these distinctive groups are the diocesan vicars forane, the pastors, the parochial vicars, the priests, the laity, the persons of a certain specified age (v. g., all between the ages of twenty-one and fifty-nine with relation to the law of fasting), etc.

In a diocese the residential bishop, the vicar-general, the ranking court official (*officialis*), and possibly also the chancellor, may well enjoy certain legal rights induced through legal custom. It is postulated however that these rights emerged, not from the repeated acts of these officials alone and apart from compulsion or assistance on the side of their subjects, but rather through the repeated acts of their subjects in matters over which one or the other of these officials has competence. For example, the later residential bishops in a diocese could not assert the legal right to an extended vacation in view of any such factual custom practiced by their predecessors. On the other hand, they could through a sufficiently protracted customary practice acquire a legal right to a semi-annual canonical visitation of all the parishes if the pastors of the diocese were willing co-operators in the repeated acts of visitation.

---

5. Canons 335, § 1; 294, § 1; 323, § 1.

Legal customs may also be induced by the diocesan curia, described in canon 363, § 1.[6] These persons in the diocese form a distinct group which is united in the bond of their common duty of assisting the ordinary in ruling the diocese. Distinctive groups within the curia also seem able to induce legal customs with regard to the matters that occasion their bond in common. The synodal judges and examiners, the parish consultors, and the notaries may be classified as such distinctive groups. However, often their concerted acts will induce not a true legal custom, but rather a *stylus curiae,* in the sense of "the mode of procedure, or the formalities customarily observed in the preparation and execution of curial business administratively or extra-judicially."[7]

Finally, the diocesan consultors as a distinct and united group may induce a legal custom. This they may do, however, only through those acts in which they function as a true community. Their inducing of a legal custom would be altogether unwarranted if they acted in concert simply as any four or six priests of the diocese, and apart from the functions performed by them as diocesan consultors. In their priestly capacity they take their place in the fuller community of the priests of the diocese.

ARTICLE 4. *The Deanery*

In accord with canon 217 each diocese is to be divided into separate districts, each of these comprising a number of parishes. These districts are called deaneries (or *vicariatus foranei, decanatus, archipresbyteratus*). At the head of each deanery is placed a priest chosen by the bishop, preferably from among the pastors of the district, and he is given the title of *vicar forane.*[8] In this office the vicar forane is to

---

6. Canon 363, § 1. — "Curia dioecesana constat illis personis quae Episcopo aliive qui, loco Episcopi, dioecesim regit, opem praestant in regimine totius dioecesis."

§ 2. — "Quare ad eam pertinent Vicarius Generalis, officialis, cancellarius, promotor iustitiae, defensor vinculi, synodales iudices et examinatores, parochi consultores, auditores, notarii, cursores et apparitores."

7. Beste, *Introductio in Codicem,* prol. 15n.

8. Canons 445 and 446.

"assist the bishop in his diocesan government, particularly through vigilance exercised over the priests of the determined district."[9]

The Catholics of a particular deanery constitute a true community, which is united in a common territory and is subject to a common presiding official, the dean of the district. There are some authors who imply that a deanery has not a capacity for inducing a legal custom by the very fact that they omit mention of it in their list of qualified communities. Among these are Cocchi, Berutti, and Augustine.[10] But among those who expressly include the deanery in their list of qualified communities are Cappello, Beste, and Michiels.[11]

The writer holds that the deanery has the ability to induce a legal custom, since one can deduce from its constitutive elements that it has a capacity for receiving ecclesiastical law. Each deanery is a canonically established and fixed subdivision of the diocese.[12] Further evidence that it has a direct relation to the common good of the episcopal jurisdiction arises from a study of the office of its head, the vicar forane. The bishop appoints the vicar forane to enlist his aid in the governing of the diocese. Beste includes the office of the vicar forane under those offices whose ordinary jurisdiction is of a vicarious character.[13] Thus in the performance of his duties he acts for the bishop and as his assistant. In accord with canon 449 he must at least once a year submit a report to the ordinary on the state of the vicariate, in which report he is among other things to suggest remedies for anything of a scandalous nature which may have arisen. In this light it is quite possible to conceive of the vicar forane as suggesting to the ordinary certain needed regulations, which the ordinary in turn may impose upon the territory by way of a common and abiding precept, i. e., after the fashion of a true law. Therefore, since the deanery has a capacity at least for receiving ecclesiastical law, it may induce a legal custom.

Of the distinctive groups of a deanery able to induce legal customs an example of the priests of the district may be offered as an illustra-

---

9. Wernz-Vidal, *Ius Canonicum,* II, 905.

10. Cf. Cocchi, *Commentarium,* I, 218; Berutti, *Institutiones,* I, 100-101; Augustine, *A Commentary on the New Code of Canon Law,* I, 109.

11. Cf. Cappello, *Summa Iuris Canonici,* I, 89; Beste, *Introductio in Codicum,* p. 95; Michiels, *Normae Generalis,* I, 142.

12. Canon 217.

13. *Introductio in Codicem,* p. 197.

tion. Wernz-Vidal suggest that an approved custom might be induced whereby the priests of the deanery elect their own vicar forane.[14]

ARTICLE 5. *The Parish*

The parish is described in canon 216, § 1, in the following manner: "The territory of each diocese shall be divided into distinct territorial parts; to each of these is to be assigned its particular church with a determined people, and at the head of each is to be placed a particular rector, as its proper pastor, for the care of souls that must there be exercised." Canon 216, § 3, designates these distinct parts or territorial divisions of the diocese as parishes. Paragraphs 2 and 3 of the same canon provide for a similar division of vicariates and prefectures apostolic, these divisions being designated as quasi-parishes. Finally, paragraph 4 of this canon indicates the need of an apostolic indult for the erecting of a parish which exclusively serves for the faithful of a different language or nationality, or of a personal or a family parish; which serves for a specific group of persons such as soldiers; or for a distinctive class of persons such as the members of regal or noble ancestry.[15] Each of these parochial units is a true community with a determined people and a proper superior, the pastor. The community is circumscribed through the element either of territory, of family lineage, of military status, of national or lingual heritage, or of these latter cumulatively with the element of territory.

The commentators are sharply divided in adjudging the capacity of the parish to induce legal customs. Among those who expressly deny that a parish has this capacity are Berutti, Cocchi, Augustine, and Coronata.[16] Among those who regard a parish as having this capacity are Beste, Michiels, Cappello, Vermeersch-Creusen, Van Hove and Regatillo.[17]

---

14. Cf. *Ius Canonicum,* II, 908.

15. Cf. Beste, *Introductio in Codicem,* p. 230.

16. Cf. Berutti, *Institutiones,* I, 101; Cocchi, *Commentarium,* I, 218; Augustine, *A Commentary on the New Code of Canon Law,* I, 109; Coronata, *Institutiones,* I, 141.

17. Cf. Beste, *Introductio in Codicem,* p. 95; Michiels, *Normae Generales,* I, 142; Cappello, *Summa Iuris Canonici,* I, 89; Vermeersch-Creusen, *Epitome,* I, 131; Van Hove, *De Consuetudine,* p. 80; Regatillo, *Institutiones Iuris Canonici,* I, 80.

The writer believes that from a study of the canonical concept of the parochial community as a single body one can rightfully conclude that a parish has the capacity for inducing legal customs. It cannot be denied that each parish community is a canonical institution which of its nature is permanent. This is clear from canon 216, which provides that all dioceses (and, where feasible, also vicariates and prefectures apostolic) shall be divided into parishes (or quasi-parishes). Thus there applies the principle, as presented in the preceding chapter, with reference to the proper determining of what constitutes a qualified community.[18]

A further study of the parochial institute may strengthen the thesis that a parish is to be considered as a qualified community. Each parish has a common good which is of great importance to the Church. The parish is the unit-cell of ecclesiastical life. Common worship and common instruction are normally conducted along parochial lines. And discipline in the Church is protected in the first line by pastors, each of whom in relation to his flock enjoys certain ordinary administrative powers in the use of which he is not to be considered simply as the vicar of the bishop. Benedict XIV made this clear in speaking of the fitness of having certain reserved cases in the diocese. In this connection he added:

> . . . ne secus Parochi conquerantur, suam ordinariam potestatem, ipsis prorsus insciis, nimis admodum coarctari.[19]

Although indeed the pastor has no power to make laws for the promotion of good order within his parish, yet the regulating of parochial activities seems to be of sufficient importance to the good of the Church to make the establishing of binding regulations permissible in some matters proper to a single parish. Legal custom could supply the binding force of true law in these instances. The vigilance of the pastor[20] and the canonical visitation of the ordinary[21] offer a sufficient safe-

---

18. Cf. *supra*, pp. 85-88.

19. Benedictus XIV, *De Synodo Dioecesana* (novissima ed., 13 Libri in 2 vols., Romae, 1783), Lib. V, c. 4, n. 3.

20. Cf. *praesertim*, canon 467.

21. Canon 343.

guard to preclude the possible inducing of particular customary law within a parish from becoming an unruly factor.

This conclusion applies not only to the ordinary parochial community, but to quasi-parishes, and also to national and personal parishes. Further arguments may be adduced in relation to the last two types of parishes. Indeed, a parish which is established under conditions that imply specific needs is to be regarded as having a capacity for receiving particular written law. National parishes normally have a local extension through a number of territorial parishes, and their people have usually been trained in a national heritage with its own particular laws and usages. These circumstances argue strongly for the capacity on the part of such parishes to become subject to some particular law for the good of the whole legislative jurisdiction of which they are a canonically established part. Again, personal parishes are of a quite unique configuration, and it may well be that the normal mode of government as obtaining in the usual parish will prove inapplicable to the well-being of the personal parish. Customary law could supply for deficiencies in the written law in this regard.

Advertence to the question of a minority group within a parish may help by contrast to clarify the capacity of a whole parochial community to induce legal customs. Often a parish will have within its boundaries a group of persons of common foreign extraction. But unless these persons constitute the major portion of the parochial community, they may not as a group be considered to have any approved status before the law. If the ordinary of the place were to erect a parish to serve their specific needs, they would then be recognized as an ecclesiastical community, that is, as persons to whom as a group there has accrued a canonical approbation. But as long as they remain only a minority group within a parochial community, their common good may not be considered to bear sufficiently on the general good of the Church to call for the establishing of regulations binding for them alone. The principle that the fact of canonical approbation helps to determine a community's capacity for inducing customary law seems a particularly satisfactory criterion in this instance.

In strict adherence to the principles proposed the writer must present the opinion that a pastor in his *public and official* acts may come to enjoy certain rights through the emergence of customary law. However, any objective rights accruing to a parochial office through customary usage must have been induced through the *common consent* of the parishioners, and not simply through prescriptive claims advanced by the pastor alone, or even by a succession of pastors. Thus, for example, a pastor may never allege that through customary law he has acquired a right to an abbreviated reading of his Sacred Office, for the recitation of the canonical hours is not a matter that comes within the purview of the common consent of the parishioners. Contrariwise, the legal regulation of certain stole fees (e. g., with reference to the administration of solemn baptism) may be determined by customary law if the common usage of the parishioners has through the requisite time, the while all other demands have been properly met (*positis ponendis*), induced a specific amount as the due offering.[22]

Often when there is a second canonically established community within the confines of a parish (e. g., a community of clerics religious or a sodality of a confraternity), regulation by law may become necessary or useful with reference to their interactivities. This need could arise with regard to the rights that touch upon the conducting of funerals, the holding of processions, the frequenting of oratories or shrines, etc. Since both communities in this case are canonically approved, the usages arising to regulate their particular interactivities may take on the force of customary law.

In addition the writer proposes that two or more parishes when acting with common consent may induce legal customs, and similarly all the parishes of a city. But those parishes which remained outside the influence that derived from a factual custom may not appropriate to themselves any right in law when the custom has been juridically induced, for "customs are not to become appropriated by one church from another even within the same diocese."[23]

It may here be proper to advert to the community of the family, which all authors agree is unable to induce a legal custom.[24] The family

22. Canon 463, § 1, seems to lend itself to this interpretation. — "Ius est parocho ad praestationes quas ei tribuit vel probata consuetudo vel legitima taxatio ad normam can. 1507, § 1."

23. Cf. *supra*, p. 60.

24. Cf. Van Hove, *De Consuetudine*, p. 76, for confirmation of this statement.

exists by natural right. Canonical approbation of the institute would be an utterly supererogatory gesture and a completely misguided act. Order in the community of the family is maintained by the dominative power of the head of the household. This mode of rule the Church has always been zealous to defend. Further, the very instability of the family precludes its ability to induce legal customs. Whatever practices may grow up within a family, or by family tradition, will be mere observances, and hence cannot take on the force of law.

ARTICLE 6. *The Collegiate Chapter*

The collegiate chapter is in a general way defined in canon 391, § 1, as a college of clerics instituted for the conducting of a more solemn worship of God in their particular church. The cathedral chapter is furthermore the senate and the counseling body of the bishop, and when the see becomes vacant it takes the place of the bishop in the ruling of the diocese until it has in accordance with the law elected a vicar to function in its name. Thus each collegiate chapter like every cathedral chapter is a canonically approved community.

A cathedral chapter may most certainly induce legal customs, for the members of the chapter are a distinctive group within the legislative jurisdiction of the diocese. The cathedral chapter is the prototype of the body of diocesan consultors, which body as the bishop's council is better known in this country.

The writer likewise maintains with the almost unanimous consent of the commentators that the collegiate chapter may induce legal customs, at least in those activities in which they are governed by law. One author, Berutti, denies this power to them. He claims that whatever customs they induce will simply be factual customs which remain devoid of legal worth.[25] However, that they have a capacity for receiving law, and indeed a law that is proper to the individual chapter, is evidenced in canon 397. That canon, relative to the right and duty of precedence within the chapter, makes the general law of the Church the binding norm, "nisi aliud in statutis capitularibus caveatur."

Wernz-Vidal designated these statutes as true law for the reason that they exist as an abiding norm and regulate the activities of a public

25. Cf. *Institutiones,* I, 101.

body.[26] Furthermore, in canons 408, § 1, and 417, § 2, there is legislation which governs certain activities of the chapters, but an express exception is made in favor of possible divergent customs. Therefore it seems rather certain that all collegiate chapters of canons may induce legal customs, at least within the ambit of their communal activities.

26. Cf. *Ius Canonicum,* II, 854.

CHAPTER X

COMMUNITIES OF RELIGIOUS

The religious state is defined in canon 487 as "a fixed and permanent mode of community life, in which the faithful (who are religious), over and above the common precepts, undertake to observe also the evangelical counsels through the vows of obedience, chastity and poverty." That congregations of religious are of importance to the common good was made clear by Pope Pius IX (1846-1878) when he described them as "those most beloved auxiliary troops of the soldiers of Christ, of the greatest use and refulgence, and a safeguard both to Christian society and to civil society."[1]

The communities of religious may be divided into three chief divisions: 1) Orders and congregations, each one distinct in itself, since it is to have its own name and habit,[2] and, what seems even more important, each one having laws proper to itself;[3] 2) Provinces, that is, canonical divisions of a religious congregation, to be composed of a union of many houses of the congregation under one superior;[4] 3) a house of religious, the least personal extension of a religious community.[5] An examination of each of these divisions of religious communities for the purpose of ascertaining their ability to induce legal customs will be made in the three articles of this chapter. A scholium will be added regarding those who live a community life apart from the profession of vows, i. e., quasi-religious, and a second scholium will be subjoined regarding lay institutes.

ARTICLE 1. *Orders and Congregations*

Societies of religious are divided in the Code first into Orders and Congregations: *Orders* are those societies whose members take solemn

1. Allocut. *Ubi primum,* 17 iun. 1847 — *Collectanea in usum secretariae S. Cong. Episcoporum et Regularium,* edita cura A. Bizzarri (Romae: ex Typographia Rev. Camerae Apostolicae, 1863), p. 868.
2. Cf. canon 492, § 3.
3. Cf. canon 488, 1°.
4. Cf. canon 488, 6°.
5. Cf. canon 488, 5°.

vows, and *Congregations* are those societies whose members profess simple vows, whether temporary or perpetual.[6] Further, a society of religious may have either a *pontifical approval,* namely when it has received at least a decree of praise from the Apostolic See, or it may have simply a *diocesan approval,* namely when it has been erected by local ordinaries but has not yet received this decree.[7] Finally, the religious society is a society of *clerical* religious, namely when the majority of its members is raised to the priesthood; otherwise the society is one of *lay* religious.[8]

A community of religious co-extensive with a whole Order or Congregation can certainly induce legal customs, for each religious society must be canonically approved and is ruled by laws proper to itself. Canon 488, 1°, states:

Venit nomine:

> *Religionis,* societas, a legitima ecclesiastica auctoritate approbata, in qua sodales, secundum *proprias ipsius societatis leges,* vota publica, perpetua vel temporaria, elapso tamen tempore renovanda, nuncupant, atque ita ad evangelicam perfectionem tendunt.

Having a capacity as a community for receiving law, Orders and Congregations fulfill the sole requirement of canon 26, and so may induce customs obtaining the force of law.

It is also true that distinct groups within an Order or Congregation may induce legal customs. Such a group, for example, is the supreme chapter of the religious institute, which is a legitimately organized body of those who have a vote on certain matters subject to deliberation and decision in the institute.[9] Another distinct group is the body of provincial superiors when discriminated from the supreme chapter; and again, the group of all the local superiors in the institute. Each of these groups, as a body, is subject to the regulations of the religious institute, and is entrusted with the task of maintaining the good order of the institute on satisfactory levels.

---

6. Cf. canon 488, 2°.
7. Cf. canon 488, 3°.
8. Cf. canon 488, 4°.
9. Cf. Schaefer, *De Religiosis ad Normam Iuris Canonici* (3. ed., Romae: S. A. L. E. R., 1940), p. 231 (hereafter cited *De Religiosis*).

ARTICLE 2. *Provinces*

A province in a religious society has been defined as a canonically established division of that society. It is composed of a number of the houses of the religious society which are united under one superior.[10] Canon 491, § 1, states that it is the Apostolic See alone which is competent to divide a religious institute of pontifical approval into provinces, to join or circumscribe the provinces already established, to establish new provinces, or to suppress the ones already established. It seems that the law of the Code does not contemplate the division of a religious institute into provinces if it has not previously received pontifical approval, since it treats only of religious institutes of pontifical approval in the aforementioned canon. Provision for the expansion of religious institutes of diocesan approval is regulated in canon 495, § 1, which states that a religious institute of diocesan approval may not establish houses in another diocese without the express permission of the ordinary of the place of the motherhouse and also of the ordinary of the diocese wherein the house is to be established.

Each province of every religious institute of pontifical approval seems certainly to have a capacity for inducing legal customs. Each province is a canonically established part of a society of religious, which is designated to have permanence, since the Apostolic See reserves to itself all authority for any change whatsoever in a province's boundaries. Each province is united under its proper superior, who by law has the title of major superior,[11] and thus exercises ordinary power in the regulation of certain activities of the religious committed to his care.[12] These various elements point to the fact that a province of religious is subject to regulation as a distinct and unified body in a lasting manner and over a rather extensive territory, and thus has a capacity for receiving ecclesiastical law which is proper to itself. Having this capacity, the province is able to induce legal customs.

10. Cf. canon 488, 6°.

11. Cf. canon 488, 8°.

12. Among these ordinary powers may be mentioned the right of canonical visitation (canon 511), the right of admitting postulants to the novitiate and subsequent religious profession (canon 543), and the right of issuing testimonial letters (canon 544).

Distinctive groups within a province of religious include for example the provincial's body of consultors,[13] and also the body of local superiors who are at the head of the various houses of the province.

Whether it can be maintained that religious institutes of diocesan approval may be discriminated into communities which are simply co-extensive with the dioceses into which they have spread (in a manner analogous to provinces in a religious institute of pontifical approval) is not quite so evident. The difficulty lies in determining whether the religious in a single diocese are sufficiently distinct from those of other dioceses to warrant a capacity for receiving their own laws. However, the writer ventures the opinion that such is the case, primarily by reason of the duties assigned to the individual ordinaries of such religious. Canon 495, § 1, orders that religious of diocesan approval may not expand into another diocese without the consent of the ordinary of the place. Once the institute is established in more than one diocese, the consent of each of the ordinaries must be obtained before any of the constitutions of the religious institute may be changed. This canon carries with it the implication that in each diocese to which a religious institute of diocesan approval may have spread there may well be need for some particular law, and therefore the complete religious institute is not to be regulated by statutes applicable primarily to only one diocese. Customs arising among such religious in one diocese could well supply for *lacunae* in the law of the constitutions, inasmuch as these were designed originally to apply only to the religious of the institute resident in the first diocese. These customs, granted the fulfillment of the rest of the conditions, should be honored as having full legal worth.

ARTICLE 3. *Single Houses of Religious*

A) The word *monasteries* in the Code points to houses of monks regular or canons regular, or also to houses of women religious professed with solemn vows (*moniales*).[14] When a monastery is further

13. Cf. canon 516, § 1.
14. Cf. Schaefer, *De Religiosis,* p. 79.

distinguished as being *sui iuris* it is regulated by laws proper to itself. This may be the case with either men or women religious, the difference being that among men the superior is vested with ordinary jurisdiction, and himself makes the laws, while among women the laws are approved by the Apostolic See, though they are proper to that one community.[15] A monastery *sui iuris* can evidently induce legal customs, since it has a capacity for receiving ecclesiastical laws proper to itself. Any monastery which is not *sui iuris* will fall under the same rules as a local religious house, which question will be treated in the succeeding division.

A conventual priory is in all respects like a monastery *sui iuris* except that it is ruled over by a prior, not by an abbot. A simple priory is a house of religious dependent upon a monastery *sui iuris* for its laws. However, the communal life in a simple priory is altogether separate from that of the monastery, and so must be regulated as a distinct unit.[16] Thus a simple priory will come under the rules for a local house, just as any monastery which is not *sui iuris*.

B) Single houses of religious are specified in the Code as houses of full juridical development if at least six professed religious dwell in the house, and at least four of these are priests in the event that the religious institute is a clerical institute.[17] By implication from this canon all other houses of religious are only of inchoate juridical development. The difference between them, as specifically implied in the Code, is that local ordinaries are to exercise more than the usual vigilance over the latter, also when they are the houses of exempt religious, lest abuses creep in or scandal arise.[18]

Each house of religious is a true community in the sense that there is present a plurality of persons, united in the bond of their communal life conducted according to the rule and constitutions of their religious institute. Further, each house must be canonically established according to the rules of canon 497, § 1. This canonical erection gives to the house a juridic capacity before the law. Evidence of this is that all houses of religious, as long as in this matter they are not excluded or

---

15. Cf. *loc. cit.*
16. Cf. Schaefer, *De Religiosis,* p. 80.
17. Cf. canon 488, 5°.
18. Cf. canon 617, § 2.

restricted through the rules or constitutions, are adjudged capable of acquiring and possessing temporal goods along with the fixed and established revenues.[19] Each house is further a distinct unit of religious obliged by their vows to live a communal life according to the regulations of the common law and the rules and constitutions of their society. Therefore it seems that all the conditions necessary to give them a capacity for receiving law are present. In that light they can induce customs which obtain the force of law.

There may appear to be some difficulty for acknowledging the nature of the communal life of an isolated house of religious as being public in character. Such a group may seem rather to resemble a family, since in their communal life they appear to be subject exclusively to the dominative power of the local superior. Yet, the vow of each religious, if it is to be a valid vow at all, must be recognized by legitimate ecclesiastical authority, and in that manner becomes a public vow.[20] Therefore the vow of obedience as professed by a religious extends to the obligation of the communal life, and is recognized as such by law. Again, in the special or particular end which each religious institute proposes to pursue — e. g., to educate, to care for the sick, even to practice the contemplative life — there is a definite relation to the public good of the Church, and this demands regulation by law.

From the practical approach one must recognize the factual difficulty for a religious house to induce a legal custom. The frequent change of administration and the vigilance exercised over religious houses militate against custom as an agency of law. The term of a local superior, who is charged with the proper administration of the house according to law, runs for only three years.[21] It would be necessary that a succession of local superiors through at least forty years co-operate benevolently in a factual custom before it could take on the force of law. Added to this consideration is that of the canonical visitation to which each house according to canon 511 is subject, and at which time all factually contravening practices of whatever type may be uprooted. Finally, the ordinary of the place is empowered to exercise certain vigilance over religious, and he may take steps to cut short all con-

19. Cf. canon 531.
20. Cf. canon 1308.
21. Cf. canon 505.

tinuance of the factual custom.[22] If however a factual custom has amid these various checks continued for the requisite or postulated duration of time, then it seems to acquire true legal force.

A novitiate must be considered in a different light in respect to its ability as a community to induce legal customs. The difference lies in the fact that novices are not according to their juridical status professed with the public vows of religion. However, according to canon 561, § 2, "novitius potestati Magistri ac Superiorum religionis subest eisque oboedire tenetur." Vermeersch-Creusen state that the master of novices enjoys over the novices a certain domestic power which he can employ in the external forum. From this it seems warranted to conclude that, if the novices of a certain religious house (or of one of its provinces) have acted consistently according to a custom of fact *with* the benevolent co-operation of the superiors charged with administering the law in the novitiate, then they too as a community are able to induce a legal custom.

ARTICLE 4. *Filial Houses*

A filial house was defined by the Sacred Congregation of Religious as one which does not constitute its own community, but is, as it were, member and part of the larger and principal house upon which it is altogether dependent. It possesses no goods of its own, and its superior is appointed and removed at the will of the superior of the larger community, who in turn governs the whole community.[23]

It can be said, then, that a filial house of religious cannot induce legal customs for want of the independent status which a community must enjoy, at least in that in which it is united, if it is to have a capacity as a community for receiving an ecclesiastical law. The Sacred Congregation itself stated that a filial house is not to be considered a community in itself (*non constituit propriam Communitatem*), and therefore it cannot be recognized as a community which has a legal capacity in itself.

---

22. Cf. canons 512, 533, 535, 603, 607, 617.

23. Cf. S. C. de Religiosis, 1 febr. 1924 — *Acta Apostolicae Sedis, Commentarium Officiale* (Romae, 1909-1929; Civitate Vaticana, 1929 —), XVI (1924), 95 (hereafter cited *AAS*).

Scholium 1. Communities of Quasi-Religious

Quasi-religious are treated in canons 673 to 681. Their societies are not religious institutes, nor are their members properly designated as religious,[24] but both the societies and their members have a true juridic status, as is evidenced in the official advertence accorded to them in these canons of the Code and in the regulations therein set down for their canonical government. Since it is necessary that these societies, their provinces, and the various houses all be canonically erected,[25] and since they are subject to regulation by constitutions approved by competent ecclesiastical authority,[26] they may be said to follow in every respect the rules that apply to true religious communities in the matter of inducing legal customs.

Scholium 2. Secular Institutes

On February 11, 1947, the present Pope Pius XII published an Apostolic Constitution entitled *Provida Mater Ecclesia.* It defined the canonical status of those "secular institutes" in which lay persons may seek Christian perfection.[27] He declared that these institutes are to have a true juridic status,[28] and to that end he decreed that the *Regulae* appended to the Constitution were to be recognized as true law and administered under the competence of the Sacred Congregation of Religious.[29]

The institutes are distinct from associations of the faithful[30] as well as from religious institutes and also societies whose members live their life in common.[31] The members are to take the three vows of evangelical counsel, but privately before God and as binding in conscience.[32] They are to have community houses, in which those who are responsible

24. Cf. canon 673, § 1.

25. Cf. canon 674.

26. Cf. canon 675.

27. Cf. *AAS,* XXXIX (1947), 114-124.

28. "... ut illa autem Instituta, quae approbationem mereantur, talem obtineant *peculiarem iuridicam ordinationem,* quae eorum naturae, finibus, adiunctis apte pleneque respondeat...." —*Ibid.,* p. 119.

29. *Loc. cit.*

30. *Lex Peculiaris Institutorum Saecularium,* Art. I—*ibid.,* p. 120.

31. Art. II, § 1—*loc. cit.*

32. Art. III, § 2, 1°, *ibid.,* p. 121.

for the regulation of the institute, both on the supreme plane and on regional planes, must live.[33] Other members need not live in a community house, though they are to convene there for spiritual exercises and other like matters.[34] Bishops may erect a secular institute as a moral person only after consultation with the Sacred Congregation of Religious.[35] The constitutions of each institute are to be well defined and approved.[36] With canonical approbation so clearly expressed, it follows that secular institutes in general as well as in each community may induce legal customs.

---

33. Art. IV, § 1 — *ibid.*, p. 122.
34. Art. IV, § 2 — *loc. cit.*
35. Art. V — *loc. cit.*
36. Art. VI — *ibid.*, pp. 122-123.

Chapter XI

ASSOCIATIONS OF THE FAITHFUL

The associations of the faithful of which the law treats in canons 684 to 725 are those which are defined in the commentaries as *ecclesiastical.* Commentators employ this term to distinguish these associations from those which are *laical,* i. e., those which have never received the positive approval of ecclesiastical authority.[1]

An ecclesiastical association may be defined generically as a voluntary union of the faithful which has as its purpose the pursuit of a particular phase of the mission of the Catholic Church. These associations are said to be of the faithful, not in the sense that they must be the exclusive property of the Catholic laity, but rather — since they are different from religious institutes and societies whose members live their life in common after the manner of religious—in the sense that the laity too may be enrolled in these associations without ceasing to be lay persons of the world. The clergy may also be enrolled in these associations, not however as clerics, but as members of the body of the faithful.[2]

Ecclesiastical associations will be treated in two articles: 1) associations of third orders secular, and 2) associations called confraternities and pious unions. In a third article will be treated the lay associations of the faithful.[3]

It is evident that only associations of the faithful merit discussion in an examination of the communities qualified for inducing customs which may obtain the force of ecclesiastical law. Any association of the type mentioned in canon 684 (those which are secret, condemned, seditious, suspect, or which are intent upon freeing themselves of the legitimate vigilance of the Church) are roundly excoriated in the law and are forbidden to the faithful.[4]

---

1. Cf. Cappello, *Summa Iuris Canonici,* II, 103 and 104.
2. Cf. Cappello, *loc. cit.*
3. For the distinction between ecclesiastical associations, that is, such as are formally erected or positively approved by ecclesiastical authority, and lay associations, that is, such as exist apart from any positive approval of ecclesiastical authority, cf. canon 686, § 1.
4. Cf. canon 684 in connection with canons 2314, § 1, 3° and 2335.

ARTICLE 1. *Associations of Third Orders Secular*

The notion of a third order secular is defined in canon 702. In the first paragraph of this canon secular tertiaries are defined as "those who in the world, under the moderation of some Order and in accordance with its spirit, strive to attain to Christian perfection in a manner that harmonizes with their secular life, and in a way that accords with the regulations approved for them by the Holy See." The second paragraph of this canon explains that if a third order secular is divided into associations, then each such lawfully established association is called a sodality of tertiaries.

Either a third order in its entirety or also each sodality of tertiaries within it can be considered a true community in the sense herein defined. Each is composed of a plurality of persons united in the common bond of seeking Christian perfection in the spirit of the Order and according to the regulations approved for them by the Holy See. Further, each sodality must be considered as a unit in itself. In canon 705 it is ordered that individual sodalities of tertiaries are to be independent of one another. And each sodality is in law constituted *ad modum corporis organici,*[5] i. e., as a collegiate body with some kind of internal regimen, usually a president and a consulting body.[6]

A third order in its entirety has with certainty the capacity for inducing legal customs, although it is difficult to conceive of the greater part of so far extended a community as acting consistently in a similar manner so that in consequence a change in the written law is thereby effected. However, since as a distinct group of persons they are the subject of statutes, proper to them and approved by the Holy See, they do have the capacity for receiving ecclesiastical laws. It is possible, therefore, that in a sufficiently long time the greater part of a third order could repeat acts of a similar nature consistently enough and with whatever intention may be necessary if a legal custom is to become established.

Each sodality of a third order is a canonically recognized body, and in that has a true juridic status.[7] If by apostolic privilege such a so-

5. Cf. Beste, *Introductio in Codicem,* p. 471.
6. Cf. *ibid.,* p. 465.
7. Cf. canon 702, § 2.

dality is established by exempt religious in any of their churches, it is exempted from the jurisdiction of the local ordinary in respect to its internal discipline and spiritual direction.[8] In this respect it is subject to the exempt clerics with whose Order it has been affiliated.[9] Finally, since canon 689, § 1, states that each association of the faithful is to have its own statutes, previously reviewed and approved by the Apostolic See or the local ordinary, it follows that each sodality of a third order has a capacity for being governed by its own laws. Cappello makes it clear that this canon regards individual sodalities as having their own statutes, for he states that it is the major superiors of those Orders which have tertiaries affiliated with them who confirm the statutes of the individual sodalities.[10] Therefore, since sodalities of tertiaries can be governed by true ecclesiastical laws, they can induce legal customs which may obtain the force of law.

ARTICLE 2. *Confraternities and Pious Unions*

Confraternities and pious unions are defined in canon 707. A pious union is an association of the faithful which is established for the exercise of some work of piety or charity; it need not be established as a sodality, i. e., *ad modum corporis organici.* A confraternity must be erected as a sodality, and it must have as an added purpose the enhancement of public worship.

These groups, too, fulfill the notion of a community, since they exist as pluralities of persons distinguishably united in the common bond of their particular ecclesiastical work. Further, they have a canonical status, either as confraternities in that they have been formally erected and have become endowed with the nature of a moral person in the Church,[11] or as pious unions in that they received at least the positive approval of ecclesiastical authority.[12] Schaefer (+1948) explained that ecclesiastical approval accords to an association of the faithful its very right of existence. Through this approbation, he added,

---

8. Cf. canon 690, § 2.
9. Cf. canon 702, § 1.
10. *Summa Iuris Canonici,* II, 106.
11. Cf. canon 708 and 687.
12. Cf. canon 708.

the association becomes recognized by the Church as a society in fact, and receives, not a juridic, but a collective personality.[13]

These associations (unless exempt by privilege) are subject to the jurisdiction and the vigilance of the local ordinary.[14] It is this immediate subjection to episcopal jurisdiction which gives evidence that these associations can be governed by law. Canon 691, § 1, makes it clear that a sodality, when canonically erected within the confines of a parish, is to be considered subject not to the ordinary power of the pastor, but to that of the local ordinary, and is to render an annual account to him. Neither the moderator nor the chaplain is contemplated in the law as able by means of dominative power alone to govern the associations. The powers expressly accorded to them are those of blessing the insignia of the association and of enrolling members, along with which they have the right and duty of seeking faculties for any extra-diocesan priest who is invited to preach to the association.[15]

Further, each sodality of a confraternity or of a pious union of the same title and institute is to be independent of all others of a similar nature,[16] and is to be ruled by its own statutes, previously reviewed and approved by the Apostolic See or the local ordinary.[17] Since, therefore, confraternities and pious unions, as well as the particular sodalities of each, are subject exclusively to the jurisdiction of the local ordinary or of the Holy See, and may be governed by their own ecclesiastically approved statutes, they may be said to have a capacity for receiving ecclesiastical law, and thus are able to induce legal customs.

Only a word need be added concerning archconfraternities and primary unions. These are simply sodalities which by apostolic indult enjoy the right of uniting with themselves other associations of the same species.[18] This unity (or aggregation) enables the united confraternities and pious unions to share in the indulgences, privileges and other spiritual benefits accorded to the archconfraternity or primary union by the Holy See. However, archconfraternities and primary

---

13. Cf. *De Religiosis,* p. 1050.
14. Cf. canon 690, § 1.
15. Cf. canons 698 and 1341.
16. Cf. canon 711.
17. Cf. canon 699, § 1.
18. Cf. canons 720 and 721.

unions gain no rights over the associations which have been joined with them.[19] Archconfraternities and primary unions, then, have no prior right to induce legal customs, but may induce them for the same reasons as confraternities and pious unions.

ARTICLE 3. *Lay Associations*

By lay associations are to be understood any associations of the faithful of whatever extension (parochial, diocesan, universal) which have not received at least the positive approval of a local ordinary or of the Apostolic See. These associations have no juridic status in the Church, for according to canon 686, § 1, "no association is recognized in the Church if it has not been erected, or at least approved, by legitimate ecclesiastical authority."

A response of the Sacred Congregation of the Council of November 13, 1920, sheds much light on the significance of canon 686. It was addressed to the Bishop of Corrientes in Argentina in answer to a difficulty regarding his jurisdiction over the lay Society of Saint Vincent de Paul in his diocese.[20] After tracing the history of the Society of St. Vincent de Paul and designating it as only a lay association, this distinction was made:

> . . . et discrimen inter laicales et ecclesiasticas (associationes) ponitur in hoc, quod in primis *non interveniat,* in aliis interveniat ad iuris effectus *auctoritas ecclesiastica,* eas per suam approbationem vel erectionem condens seu esse ecclesiasticum eis tribuens.[21]

The response continued:

> Immo absolute potest vere dici, quod sicut singuli fideles iurisdictioni Episcopi subsunt, ita manent huius iurisdictioni subiecti, quando in Societates uniuntur. Quamquam enim Episcopus ex hoc solo facto societatem vi suae iurisdictionis dirigere nequit, quemadmodum societates proprie ecclesiasticas et confraternitates dirigit, *ius tamen habet et obligationem invigilandi* ne abusus irrepant neve fideles occasione societatum ruinam salutis incurrant.[22]

19. Cf. canon 722.
20. Cf. *AAS,* XIII (1921), 135-144.
21. *Ibid.,* p. 139.
22. *Ibid.,* p. 140.

Schaefer pointed to this response, and then in explanation of the jurisdictional power of the local ordinary over such lay associations stated: "... nec *qua tales* [i. e., tamquam associationes laicales] pro suo speciali fine Ordinariis locorum subduntur."[23]

Therefore it seems clear that these lay associations of whatever nature are not *qua tales* subject to the jurisdiction of ecclesiastical authority. They are associations established by private persons and regulated by conventional pacts entered into by agreement on the part of the members. They are subject only to the vigilance of the ordinary, and unless he need impose a penal sanction, they are not subject to him in "their existence, constitution, organization, statutes, activities and internal rule."[24]

In the juridic structure of the Church, then, the existence of these lay associations is not adverted to. Juridically they are not regarded as different from any private club whose membership consists exclusively of Catholics. The writer concludes that as associations they have no capacity for receiving ecclesiastical law, and in consequence are not able to induce legal customs. Inasmuch as they are not incorporated into the structure of the Church through some canonical approbation, it cannot be said that they bear sufficiently on the good of the Church to call for regulation by law.

23. Cf. *De Religiosis*, p. 1044.
24. *AAS*, XIII (1921), 140.

CHAPTER XII

INSTITUTIONS

Final consideration will be given in two articles to those institutions of the Church which are dedicated to charitable or religious purposes. The constitution and the regulation of these institutions as non-collegiate moral persons, the subject-matter of canons 1489-1494, will receive consideration in the first article. The discipline of educational institutions as set down for seminaries in Title XXI of Book Three of the Code, and for other schools in Title XXII of the same Book of the Code, will receive study in the second article.

Persons who pertain to communities served by these institutions may be classified as: 1) those who are charged with the administration of the institution, and 2) those who derive benefit from the particular purpose of the institution (e. g., patients in a hospital, students in a school).

ARTICLE 1. *Administrators of Institutions*

All institutions may be classified as lay or ecclesiastical institutions. Beste defines the lay institute thus:

> . . . si competens superior ecclesiasticus numquam intervenerit, sive auctoritative ea erigendo tempore fundationis sive ea postea approbando, ac proinde *nullum esse* ab Ecclesia habeant, etsi forte a clericis, qua personis privatis, condita sint vel regantur.[1]

An institution is ecclesiastical, "si intercesserit erectio vel saltem approbatio auctoritatis ecclesiasticae."[2]

Even as with lay associations of the faithful, lay institutions are not contemplated in the law as having a juridic capacity. But the opposite is true of ecclesiastical institutions. They may be formally erected as non-collegiate moral persons, the subject of rights and obligations before the law,[3] or they may be erected as a trust of a collegiate body,

1. *Introductio in Codicem,* p. 735.
2. *Loc. cit.*
3. Cf. canons 1489, § 1; 99; 100.

for example, of a community of religious.[4] According to the norm of canon 1489, § 1, the administration of these institutes is to be regulated by the specifications contained in the charter of their foundation (*tabulae fundationis*). This charter is to describe the "constitution of the institute, its end, support, administration and rule, its use of income and the matter of succession to its goods in the event of its extinction."[5] Wernz-Vidal pointed to this charter as constituting the supreme law for the foundation,[6] and Cappello describes it as the *ius speciale instituti.*[7]

Accordingly, the administration of these institutions is determined by true ecclesiastical law. However, only when the administration of such ecclesiastical institutions is entrusted to a board of directors or to a chapter, all of whose members enjoy the right of a definitive vote, does there appear to be a community of persons which has the capacity for receiving law in the sense that it is charged as a body with the administration of an ecclesiastical institute. In this light such a community of persons seems able to induce legal customs. If an institution were entrusted to one sole administrator, he could of course acquire certain subjective rights through the agency of legal prescription, but as an individual it would be impossible for him to induce a legal custom.

Other community members served by charitable institutions (students in educational institutes will be discussed in the next article) consist of the patients, the inmates, or the boarders, depending upon the type of institution. It seems that this community of persons is not to be considered canonically as having a capacity for receiving ecclesiastical law. The writer prefers the interpretation that each person entering a charitable institution of the Church makes with its administrators a private contract, whereby he agrees to subject himself to the regulations of the institute in order to attain the benefits of it. In this manner, by a conventional pact, the person submits himself to the dominative power of the administrator and thus becomes subject to his precepts. No regulation by ecclesiastical law seems necessary for the good order

4. Cf. Beste, *Introductio in Codicem,* p. 736.
5. Cf. canon 1490, § 1.
6. *Ius Canonicum,* IV, Pars II, 262.
7. *Summa Iuris Canonici,* II, 541.

of the communal life of those who are served in or by such an institution. These persons do not constitute a community which can be considered rightly to have the capacity for inducing legal customs.

ARTICLE 2. *Particular Communities in Educational Institutions*

The educational institutions of the Church can be classified as parochial and diocesan schools, colleges, seminaries and universities. Neither the faculty nor the students in a parochial school seem to form a community which has the capacity for receiving ecclesiastical law. Wernz-Vidal pointed out that the local ordinary has a very grave duty to provide for the adequate inspection and regulation of the religious instruction offered in parochial schools, "secundum normas in statutis dioecesanis stabilitas."[8] Yet, no particular parochial school needs to have its own proper statutes. The writer is rather of the opinion that the communal activities of a parochial school are to be regulated by the dominative power of the pastor, that a parochial school cannot be considered as having any capacity for receiving ecclesiastical law, and hence cannot induce a legal custom. The parochial school is simply an adjunct of the parochial community; it does not form a distinctive group within the parochial community.

However, in a diocese wherein according to a decree of the III Plenary Council of Baltimore (1884) there exists a Diocesan Commission of Examiners composed of a number of priests, this board in its official capacity could induce legal customs.[9]

The administrative board and the faculty of a diocesan school, on the contrary, should be judged to have a capacity for receiving law, and hence should be regarded as able to induce legal customs. Such a school exists independently of parochial power, and even if a local ordinary had not enacted any specific statutes for the governing of its activities, such a school may nevertheless be considered as having a capacity for receiving ecclesiastical law.

The administrative board and the faculty of a Catholic college have an equal right to induce legal customs, provided that the college has

---

8. *Ius Canonicum,* IV, Pars II, 82.

9. Cf. *Acta et Decreta Concilii Plenarii Baltimorensis Tertii, A. D. 1884* (Baltimorae: J. Murphy et Soc., 1886), tit. VI, n. 203.

received the official approval of competent ecclesiastical authority, so that it is not merely a lay institution.

The juridic capacity of the authorities of a Catholic university is determined in canon 1376 and in an apostolic constitution of Pius XI entitled *Deus Scientiarum Dominus,* issued on May 24, 1931.[10] Canon 1376, § 1, states that a Catholic university of studies with its respective schools (*facultates*) can be established canonically only by the Holy See. Paragraph 2 of this canon adds that such a Catholic university and each of its schools must have its proper statutes approved by the Holy See. In article 5 of the *Deus Scientiarum Dominus* Pius XI reiterated this requisite. Article 15 states that the Rector Magnificus of the University and each of the Deans of the various schools is to have his counseling body. Article 17 states that any other authorities of the University are to be so specified in the statutes of the University. Finally article 19 speaks of the right of full professors to be inducted with full and firm right into the *collegium professorum.* Each of these collegiate bodies, then, within a Catholic university have a juridic status, and appear to have a capacity for receiving ecclesiastical law in that they are the subject of the remaining statutes of the *Deus Scientiarum Dominus.*

Finally, the ruling body of a seminary may induce legal customs.[11] Canon 1357, § 3, states that each seminary is to have its own laws, approved by the bishop. While interdiocesan or regional seminaries are to be regulated by the norms of the Holy See,[12] this does not deprive the individual seminary from receiving its particular laws.[13] The governing body of the seminary is to consist of the bishop,[14] the rector, the faculty, the econome, two ordinary confessors (these, however, particularly for the internal forum), and a spiritual director.[15] There are also to be two bodies of deputies, each to consist of two priests, the one body together with the bishop, looking after matters of discipline, the other

10. Cf. *AAS,* XXIII (1931), 241-262.
11. Cf. Beste, *Introductio in Codicem,* p. 95.
12. Cf. canon 1357, § 4.
13. Cf. Vermeersch-Creusen, *Epitome,* II, 480.
14. Cf. canon 1357.
15. Cf. canon 1358.

supervising the administration of the temporal goods.[16] This group in its entirety may be considered as a community able to induce legal customs, and within the group any distinctive part seems able to induce legal customs by means of repeated public acts performed within the scope of their office.

Further, the writer is of the opinion that a community of seminarians is able to induce legal customs. They are an altogether distinctive ecclesiastical group, united in their common aspiring to the priesthood. Their behavior and studies are regulated by law.[17] However, many of the practices peculiar to one or other seminary may not be considered as having legal worth. They are rather to be regarded as traditions of the seminary, observances altogether private in nature, and having no relation to the public good, which ever remains a determining factor for the emergence of any true law.

Thus is concluded the treatment of the particular communities which have a capacity for inducing customary law. The reader may well have noted that the element of canonical approbation in one or another form has played a common rôle for all the communities which the writer regarded as qualified for inducing a legal custom. If with reference to particular communities the writer proposed additional arguments which seemed to abstract from the universally applicable argument that would have sufficed in itself, he did so with a view to corroborating and confirming what was fundamentally established through the fact of the bestowal of approbation on the part of the competent ecclesiastical authority.

16. Cf. canon 1359.

17. Cf. canons 1367 and 1369.

CONCLUSIONS

1) Custom in both the Roman and the Canon Law is to be viewed as partaking of the nature of law. An examination of any phase of custom must be founded in a comparison with juridically binding law.

2) A community is a plurality or a group of persons, readily distinguishable as a moral unit by reason of a common bond, wherein nonetheless each person retains his individuality and is responsible for his individual actions.

3) A community may be considered collectively, i. e., as the sum-total of the members composing it. It may also be considered distributively, i. e., as composed of distinctive classes of persons.

4) Any community judged capable of inducing customary law may act to induce such a law either collectively or distributively. These latter classes of persons must be distinctive by reason of office or state of life, each bearing in some manner on the good of the community.

5) Individual persons who occupy an office recognized in the law may enjoy rights through legal custom, provided that these rights have accrued to the office through the common consent of the community.

6) Those communities whose right regulation is of sufficient importance to the common good of the Church are to be judged capable of inducing customary law. Their importance to the common good of the Church is to be judged sufficient when canonical approbation has been accorded them.

7) Canonical approbation of a given community arises through the canonical erection or canonical recognition of the community in question. Canonical approbation may be accorded a community only by an ordinary, and by no authority inferior to him.

8) Two or more canonically approved communities have the capacity of determining their interrelations with juridic effect through customary law.

9) It is the writer's opinion that customary law can be induced in a deanery, in a parish, in a quasi-parish, and in a national or a personal parish. A minor segment of a parish community cannot induce customary law, even to bind only its own members.

10) It is the writer's opinion that: a) customary law can be induced in all religious provinces, within a single diocese by religious of dioc-

esan approval, in single houses of religious and in a novitiate (with the co-operation of the superiors), but that customary law cannot be induced in filial houses of religious;

b) lesser communities of quasi-religious and of secular institutes are to be judged in this matter by the same rules that obtain for religious.

11) a) The writer considers it certain that customary law can be induced by canonically approved third orders secular and by confraternities and pious unions in their total membership.

b) It is the writer's opinion that single sodalities of ecclesiastical associations of the faithful can induce customary law, but that no lay association of the faithful, i. e., one without canonical approbation, can induce legal customs. Associations condemned by ecclesiastical authority certainly cannot induce customary law.

12) It is the writer's opinion that: a) customary law can be induced in ecclesiastical charitable institutions by an administrative board of at least three, but not by the patients;

b) in a parochial school system only a diocesan commission of examiners is to be judged capable of inducing customary law;

c) in a diocesan school, in a college, or in a university, the administrative board and the faculty along with each of these latter's affiliated schools is to be judged capable of inducing legal customs, provided only that the particular institution is canonically approved;

d) the superiors in a seminary, and also the students in cooperation with the superiors, are to be judged capable of inducing legal customs.

BIBLIOGRAPHY

Sources

Acta Apostolicae Sedis, Commentarium Officiale, Romae, 1909 ——.

Acta et Decreta Concilii Plenarii Baltimorensis Tertii, A.D. 1884, Baltimorae: Typis Joannis Murphy et Sociorum, 1886.

Acta Sanctae Sedis, 41 vols., Romae, 1865-1908.

Codex Iuris Canonici Pii X Pontificis Maximi iussu digestus, Benedicti Papae XV auctoritate promulgatus, Romae: Typis Polyglottis Vaticanis, 1917.

Collectanea in usum Secretariae Sacrae Congregationis Episcoporum et Regularium, cura A. Bizzarri edita, Romae: ex Typographia Rev. Camerae Apostolicae, 1863.

Corpus Iuris Civilis, 3 vols., Berolini: apud Weidmanus, 1928-1929. *Institutiones,* quas recognovit P. Krueger, ed. stereotypa 15., 1928; *Digesta,* quae recognovit T. Mommsen, retractavit P. Krueger, ed. stereotypa 15., 1928; *Codex Iustinianus,* quem recognovit et retractavit P. Krueger, ed. stereotypa 10., 1929; *Novellae,* quas recognovit R. Schoell, et absolvit G. Kroll, ed. stereotypa 5., 1928.

Decreta Authentica Congregationis Sacrorum Rituum, ab A. Gardellini collecta, cura H. Capalti edita, 3. ed., 4 vols., cum Supplementis usque ad annum 1888, Romae, 1856-1888.

Decretales D. Gregorii Papae IX, una cum glossis restitutae, 2 vols., Romae, 1582.

Decretum Gratiani emendatum et notationibus illustratum una cum glossis, 2 vols., Romae, 1582.

Jaffé, P., *Regesta Pontificum Romanorum ab condita Ecclesia ad annum post Christum annum 1198,* ed. secundam correctam et auctam auspiciis Gulielmi Wattenbach curaverunt S. Loewenfeld, F. Kaltenbrunner, P. Ewald, 2 vols. in 1, Lipsiae, 1885-1888.

Mansi, J. D., *Sacrorum Conciliorum Nova et Amplissima Collectio,* 53 vols. in 60, Paris-Arnhem-Leipzig, 1901-1927.

Potthast, Augustus, *Regesta Pontificum Romanorum inde ab A. post Christum natum MCXCVIII ad A. MCCCIV,* 2 vols., Berolini, 1874-1875.

Schema codicis Iuris Canonici Sanctissimi Domini Nostri Pii Papae X, cum notis Petri Card. Gasparri, 2 vols., Vol. I, Romae: Typis Polyglottis Vaticanis, 1912.

Thesaurus Resolutionum Sacrae Congregationis Concilii, 167 vols., Romae, 1718-1908.

Reference Works

Aquinas, S. Thomas, *Summa Theologica,* ed. Marietti, 6 vols., Taurini-Romae: Marietti, 1937.

Augustine, Charles, *A Commentary on the New Code of Canon Law,* 8 vols., Vol. I, 3. ed., St. Louis, Mo.: B. Herder Book Co., 1920.

Barbosa, Augustinus, *Collectanea Doctorum tam veterum quam recentiorum in Ius Pontificium Universum,* 6 vols., Lugduni, 1669.

Bauduin, J., *De Consuetudine in Iure Canonico,* Lovanii, 1888.

Belorgey, Julius, *De Consuetudine, Dissertatio Canonica,* Locagiaci: Abbatiae St. Martini, 1893.

Benedictus XIV, *De Synodo Dioecesana,* novissima ed., 13 Libri in 2 vols., Romae, 1783.

Berutti, Christopherus, *Institutiones Iuris Canonici,* 6 vols., Vol. I, Taurini-Romae: Ex Officina Libraria Marietti, 1936.

Beste, Uldaricus, *Introductio in Codicem,* 3. ed., Collegeville, Minn.: St. John's Abbey Press, 1946.

Böckhn, Placidus, *Ius Canonicum Universum,* 3 vols., Salisburgi, Parisiis, 1776.

Bouix, Dominicus, *Tractatus de Principiis Juris Canonici,* 3. ed., Parisiis, 1882.

Cappello, Felix, *Summa Iuris Canonici,* 3 vols., Vols. I-II, 3 ed., Romae: Apud Aedes Universitatis Gregorianae, 1940-1945.

———, *Summa Iuris Publici Ecclesiastici,* ed. altera, Romae: Apud Aedes Universitatis Gregorianae, 1928.

Chelodi, Io., *Ius Canonicum de Personis,* 3. ed., curavit P. Ciprotti, Vicenza: Società Anonima Tipografica, 1942.

Cicognani, Amleto, *Canon Law,* Authorized English Version by J. M. O'Hara and F. Brennan, 2. ed., Philadelphia: Dolphin Press, 1935: Reprint, Westminster, Md.: Newman Book Shop, 1947.

Cocchi, Guidus, *Commentarium in Codicem Iuris Canonici,* 8 vols. in 5, Vol. I, 5. ed., Taurinorum Augustae: Marietti, 1938.

Coronata, Matthaeus a Conte, *Institutiones Iuris Canonici,* 5 vols., Vol. I, Romae: Marietti, 1943.

De Angelis, Philippus, *Praelectiones Iuris Canonici,* 5 vols. in 9, Romae: Della Pace, 1877-1891.

De Luca, J. B., *Theatrum Veritatis et Justitiae,* 15 vols. in 9, Coloniae Agrippinae, 1706.

Devoti, Ioannes, *Tractatus Iuris Canonici Universi Publici et Privati,* 3 vols., Romae, 1803-1815.

Fagnanus, Prosper, *Commentaria in Quinque Libros Decretalium,* 4 vols., Venetiis, 1696.

Falco, Mario, *Introduzione allo Studio del "Codex Iuris Canonici,"* Torino: Fratelli Bocca, 1925.

Guilfoyle, Merlin, *Custom,* The Catholic University of America Canon Law Studies, n. 105, Washington, D. C.: The Catholic University of America, 1937.

Hostiensis, Cardinalis (Henricus de Segusio), *Summa Aurea,* Lugduni, 1568.

Ioannes Andreae, *Commentaria Novella in Quinque Libros Decretalium,* Venetiis, 1581.

Kilcullen, Th., *The Collegiate Moral Person as Party Litigant,* The Catholic University of America Canon Law Studies, n. 251, Washington, D. C.: The Catholic University of America Press, 1947.

Michiels, Gommarus, *Normae Generales Iuris Canonici,* 2 vols., Lublin, Poloniae: Universitas Catholica, 1929.

Ojetti, Benedictus, *Commentarium in Codicem Iuris Canonici,* 4 vols., Vol. I, Romae: Apud Aedes Universitatis Gregorianae, 1927.

Panormitanus, Abbas (Nicolaus de Tudeschis), *Commentaria in Quinque Libros Decretalium,* 5 vols. in 7, Venetiis, 1588.

Phillips, G., *Du Droit Ecclesiastique,* traduit par J. P. Crouzet, 2. ed., 3 vols., Paris; Le Coffre, 1833.

Pirhing, Enricus, *Ius Canonicum in V Libros Decretalium,* ed. novissima, 4 vols., Dilingae, 1722.

Regatillo, E., *Institutiones Iuris Canonici,* 2 vols., Vol. I, Santander: Sal Terrae, 1946.

Reiffenstuel, Anacletus, *Ius Canonicum Universum,* 5 vols. in 7, Parisiis, 1864-1870.

Rufinus, *Die Summa Decretorum des Magister Rufinus,* ed. Heinrich Singer, Paderborn, 1902.

Schaefer, Timotheus, *De Religiosis ad Normam Iuris Canonici,* 3 ed., Romae: S. A. L. E. R., 1940.

Schmalzgrueber, Franciscus, *Ius Ecclesiasticum Universum,* 5 vols. in 12, Romae, 1843-1845.

Sipos, Stephanus, *Enchiridion Iuris Canonici,* Pécs: Ex Typographia "Haladas R. T.," 1926.

Suárez, Franciscus, *Opera Omnia,* 28 vols., ed. Vivès, Parisiis, 1856-1861. Vols. V-VI, *De Legibus et Legislatore Deo.*

Toso, A., *Ad Codicem Iuris Canonici... Commentaria Minora,* 5 vols., Vol. I, 2. ed., Taurini-Romae: P. Marietti, 1921.

Van Hove, A., *Commentarium Lovaniense in Codicem Iuris Canonici,* Vol. I, Tom. I, *Prolegomena,* 2. ed., Mechliniae-Romae: H. Dessain, 1945; Tom. III, *De Consuetudine, De Temporis Supputatione,* Mechliniae-Romae: H. Dessain, 1933.

Vermeersch, A.-Creusen, J., *Epitome Iuris Canonici,* 3 vols., Vol. I, 6. ed., 1937, Vol. II, 6. ed., 1940, Mechliniae-Romae: H. Dessain.

Wehrlé, R., *De la Coutume dans le Droit Canonique,* Paris: Librairie du Recueil Sirey, 1928.

Wernz, Franciscus, *Ius Decretalium,* 2. ed., 6 vols., Romae et Prati, 1906-1913.

Wernz, F.-Vidal, P., *Ius Canonicum,* 7 vols. in 8, Romae: Apud Aedes Universitatis Gregorianae; Vol. I, 1938; Vol. II, 3 ed., a P. Philippo Aguirre recognita, 1943; Vol. IV, Pars I, 1934; Vol. IV, Pars II, 1935.

Articles

Couly, Aug., "La Coutume en Droit Canonique," *Le Canoniste,* Paris, 1924-1926, XLVIII (1926), 428-441.

Kinane, J., "The Community Capable of Introducing Custom," *The Irish Ecclesiastical Record,* Dublin, 1864 —, XXXVII (1937), 523-524.

Medici, G. C., "Presuppositi giustinianei d'una expressione canonistica, 'Communitas Legis Recipiendae Capax,' " *Acta Congressus Iuridici Internationalis,* 5 vols., Romae: Apollinare, 1935-1937, Vol. IV, 121-133.

ABBREVIATIONS

AAS — *Acta Apostolicae Sedis.*

ASS — *Acta Sanctae Sedis.*

C. — *Codex Iustinianus.*

D. — *Digest.*

Inst. — *Institutiones.*

Jaffé — *Regesta Pontificum Romanorum ad annum MCXCVIII.*

Mansi — *Sacrorum Conciliorum Nova et Amplissima Collectio.*

Potthast — *Regesta Pontificum Romanorum ab anno MCXCVIII ad annum MCCCIV.*

S. C. C. — Sacra Congregatio Concilii.

S. C. de Religiosis — Sacra Congregatio de Religiosis.

S. C. Ep. et Reg. — Sacra Congregatio Episcoporum et Regularium.

S. C. R. — Sacra Congregatio Rituum.

Thesaurus — *Thesaurus Resolutionum Sacrae Congregationis Concilii.*

BIOGRAPHICAL NOTE

John Patrick Cook was born on December 7, 1921, in Racine, Wisconsin. He received his grammar school education in the public schools of New Rochelle, New York, and his high school education at William Hall High School in West Hartford, Connecticut. After one year at the College of the Holy Cross in Worcester, Massachusetts, and a second year at Saint Thomas Seminary in Bloomfield, Connecticut, he entered Saint Mary's Seminary in Baltimore, Maryland. From this institution he received the A. B. and S. T. B. degrees. He was ordained to the Sacred Priesthood in Hartford, Connecticut, on December 22, 1945. In September of 1946 he enrolled in the School of Canon Law of the Catholic University of America, where he received the Baccalaureate degree in Canon Law in June of 1947, and the Licentiate degree in Canon Law in June of 1948.

ALPHABETICAL INDEX

CANON LAW STUDIES *

1. FRERIKS, REV. CELESTINE A., C. PP. S., J. C. D., Religious Congregations in Their External Relations, 121 pp., 1916.
2. GALLIHER, REV. DANIEL M., O. P., J. C. D., Canonical Elections, 117 pp., 1917.
3. BORKOWSKI, REV. AURELIUS L., O. F. M., J. C. D., De Confraternitatibus Ecclesiasticis, 136 pp., 1918.
4. CASTILLO, REV. CAYO, J. C. D., Disertación Historico-Canonica sobre la Potestad del Cabildo en Sede Vacante o Impedida del Vicario Capitular, 99 pp., 1919 (1918).
5. KUBELBECK, REV. WILLIAM J., S. T. B., J. C. D., The Sacred Penitentiaria and Its Relation to Faculties of Ordinaries and Priests, 129 pp., 1918.
6. PETROVITS, REV. JOSEPH, J. C., S. T. D., J. C. D., The New Church Law on Matrimony, X-461 pp., 1919.
7. HICKEY, REV. JOHN J., S. T. B., J. C. D., Irregularities and Simple Impediments in the New Code of Canon Law, 100 pp., 1920.
8. KLEKOTKA, REV. PETER J., S. T. B., J. C. D., Diocesan Consultors, 179 pp., 1920.
9. WANENMACHER, REV. FRANCIS, J. C. D., The Evidence in Ecclesiastical Procedure Affecting the Marriage Bond, 1920 (Printed 1935).
10. GOLDEN, REV. HENRY FRANCIS, J. C. D., Parochial Benefices in the New Code, IV-119 pp., 1921 (Printed 1925).
11. KOUDELKA, REV. CHARLES J., J. C. D., Pastors, Their Rights and Duties According to the New Code of Canon Law, 211 pp., 1921.
12. MELO, REV. ANTONIUS, O. F. M., J. C. D., De Exemptione Regularium, X-188 pp., 1921.
13. SCHAAF, REV. VALENTINE THEODORE, O. F. M., S. T. B., J. C. D., The Cloister, X-180 pp., 1921.
14. BURKE, REV. THOMAS JOSEPH, S. T. D., J. C. D., Competence in Ecclesiastical Tribunals, IV-117 pp., 1922.
15. LEECH, REV. GEORGE LEO, J. C. D., A Comparative Study of the Constitution "Apostolicae Sedis" and the "Codex Juris Canonici," 179 pp., 1922.
16. MOTRY, REV. HUBERT LOUIS, S. T. D., J. C. D., Diocesan Faculties According to the Code of Canon Law, II-167 pp., 1922.
17. MURPHY, REV. GEORGE LAWRENCE, J. C. D., Delinquencies and Penalties in the Administration and the Reception of the Sacraments, IV-121 pp., 1923.
18. O'REILLY, REV. JOHN ANTHONY, S. T. B., J. C. D., Ecclesiastical Sepulture in the New Code of Canon Law, II-129 pp., 1923.

*All published numbers are available from the Catholic University of America Press, 620 Michigan Ave., N. E., Washington, D. C., except the following: nos. 1-114 inclusive, 116, 118, 120, 121, 122, 123, 136, 153, 162, 182 and 198. But the following numbers, now reissued, are obtainable from *The Jurist*, The Catholic University of America, Washington 17, D. C., namely: nos. 5, 7, 11, 17, 18, 19, 26, 28, 30, 31, 34, 42, 44, 51, 52 and 61.

19. Michalicka, Rev. Wenceslas Cyrill, O. S. B., J. C. D., Judicial Procedure in Dismissal of Clerical Exempt Religious, 107 pp., 1923.
20. Dargin, Rev. Edward Vincent, S. T. B., J. C. D., Reserved Cases According to the Code of Canon Law, IV-103 pp., 1924.
21. Godfrey, Rev. John A., S. T. B., J. C. D., The Right of Patronage According to the Code of Canon Law, 153 pp., 1924.
22. Hagedorn, Rev. Francis Edward, J. C. D., General Legislation on Indulgences, II-154 pp., 1924.
23. King, Rev. James Ignatius, J. C. D., The Administration of the Sacraments to Dying Non-Catholics, V-141 pp., 1924.
24. Winslow, Rev. Francis Joseph, O. F. M., J. C. D., Vicars and Prefects Apostolic, IV-149 pp., 1924.
25. Correa, Rev. Jose Servelion, S. T. L., J. C. D., La Potestad Legislativa de la Iglesia Catolica, IV-127 pp., 1925.
26. Dugan, Rev. Henry Francis, A. M., J. C. D., The Judiciary Department of the Diocesan Curia, 87 pp., 1925.
27. Keller, Rev. Charles Frederick, S. T. B., J. C. D., Mass Stipends, 167 pp., 1925.
28. Paschang, Rev. John Linus, J. C. D., The Sacramentals According to the Code of Canon Law, 129 pp., 1925.
29. Piontek, Rev. Cyrillus, O. F. M., S. T. B., J. C. D., De Indulto Exclaustrationis necnon Saecularizationis, XIII-289 pp., 1925.
30. Kearney, Rev. Richard Joseph, S. T. B., J. C. D., Sponsors at Baptism According to the Code of Canon Law, IV-127 pp., 1925.
31. Bartlett, Rev. Chester Joseph, A. M., LL. B., J. C. D., The Tenure of Parochial Property in the United States of America, V-108 pp., 1926.
32. Kilker, Rev. Adrian Jerome, J. C. D., Extreme Unction, V-425 pp., 1926.
33. McCormick, Rev. Robert Emmett, J. C. D., Confessors of Religious, VIII-266 pp., 1926.
34. Miller, Rev. Newton Thomas, J. C. D., Founded Masses According to the Code of Canon Law, VII-93 pp., 1926.
35. Roelker, Rev. Edward G., S. T. D., J. C. D., Principles of Privilege According to the Code of Canon Law, XI-166 pp., 1926.
36. Bakalarczyk, Rev. Richardus, M. I. C., J. U. D., De Novitiatu, VIII-208 pp., 1927.
37. Pizzuti, Rev. Lawrence, O. F. M., J. U. L., De Parochis Religiosis, 1927 (Not Printed).
38. Bliley, Rev. Nicholas Martin, O. S. B., J. C. D., Altars According to the Code of Canon Law, XIX-132 pp., 1927.
39. Brown, Mr. Brendan Francis, A. B., LL. M., J. U. D., The Canonical Juristic Personality with Special References to its Status in the United States of America, V-212 pp., 1927.

40. CAVANAUGH, REV. WILLIAM THOMAS, C. P., J. U. D., The Reservation of the Blessed Sacrament, VIII-101 pp., 1927.
41. DOHENY, REV. WILLIAM J., C. S. C., A. B., J. U. D., Church Property: Modes of Acquisition, X-118 pp., 1927.
42. FELDHAUS, REV. ALOYSIUS H., C. PP. S., J. C. D., Oratories, IX-141 pp., 1927.
43. KELLY, REV. JAMES PATRICK, A. B., J. C. D., The Jurisdiction of the Simple Confessor, X-208 pp., 1927.
44. NEUBERGER, REV. NICHOLAS J., J. C. D., Canon 6 or the Relation of the Codex Juris Canonici to the Preceding Legislation, V-95 pp., 1927.
45. O'KEEFE, REV. GERALD MICHAEL, J. C. D., Matrimonial Dispensations, Powers of Bishops, Priests, and Confessors, VIII-232 pp., 1927.
46. QUIGLEY, REV. JOSEPH A. M., A. B., J. C. D., Condemned Societies, 139 pp., 1927.
47. ZAPLOTNIK, REV. JOHANNES LEO, J. C. D., De Vicariis Foraneis, X-142 pp., 1927.
48. DUSKIE, REV. JOHN ALOYSIUS, A. B., J. C. D., The Canonical Status of the Orientals in the United States, VIII-196 pp., 1928.
49. HYLAND, REV. FRANCIS EDWARD, J. C. D., Excommunication, Its Nature, Historical Development and Effects, VIII-181 pp., 1928.
50. REINMANN, REV. GERALD JOSEPH, O. M. C., J. C. D., The Third Order Secular of Saint Francis, 201 pp., 1928.
51. SCHENK, REV. FRANCIS J., J. C. D., The Matrimonial Impediments of Mixed Religion and Disparity of Cult, XVI-318 pp., 1929.
52. COADY, REV. JOHN JOSEPH, S. T. D., J. U. D., A. M., The Appointment of Pastors, VIII-150 pp., 1929.
53. KAY, REV. THOMAS HENRY, J. C. D., Competence in Matrimonial Procedure, VIII-164 pp., 1929.
54. TURNER, REV. SIDNEY JOSEPH, C. P., J. U. D., The Vow of Poverty, XLIX-217 pp., 1929.
55. KEARNEY, REV. RAYMOND A., A. B., S. T. D., J. C. D., The Principles of Delegation, VII-149 pp., 1929.
56. CONRAN, REV. EDWARD JAMES, A. B., J. C. D., The Interdict, V-163 pp., 1930.
57. O'NEILL, REV. WILLIAM H., J. C. D., Papal Rescripts of Favor, VII-218 pp., 1930.
58. BASTNAGEL, REV. CLEMENT VINCENT, J. U. D., The Appointment of Parochial Adjutants and Assistants, XV-257 pp., 1930.
59. FERRY, REV. WILLIAM A., A. B., J. C. D., Stole Fees, V-136 pp., 1930.
60. COSTELLO, REV. JOHN MICHAEL, A. B., J. C. D., Domicile and Quasi-Domicile, VII-201 pp., 1930.
61. KREMER, REV. MICHAEL NICHOLAS, A. B., S. T. B., J. C. D., Church Support in the United States, VI-136 pp., 1930.

62. ANGULO, REV. LUIS, C. M., J. C. D., Legislación de la Iglesia sobre la intención en la applicación de la Santa Misa, VII-104 pp., 1931.
63. FREY, REV. WOLFGANG NORBERT, O. S. B., A. B., J. C. D., The Act of Religious Profession, VIII-174 pp., 1931.
64. ROBERTS, REV. JAMES BRENDAN, A. B., J. C. D., The Banns of Marriage, XIV-140 pp., 1931.
65. RYDER, REV. RAYMOND ALOYSIUS, A. B., J. C. D., Simony, IX-151 pp., 1931.
66. CAMPAGNA, REV. ANGELO, PH. D., J. U. D., Il Vicario Generale del Vescovo, VII-205 pp., 1931.
67. COX, REV. JOSEPH GODFREY, A. B., J. C. D., The Administration of Seminaries, VI-124 pp., 1931.
68. GREGORY, REV. DONALD J., J. U. D., The Pauline Privilege, XV-165 pp., 1931.
69. DONOHUE, REV. JOHN F., J. C. D., The Impediment of Crime, VII-110 pp., 1931.
70. DOOLEY, REV. EUGENE A., O. M. I., J. C. D., Church Law on Sacred Relics, IX-143 pp., 1931.
71. ORTH, REV. CLEMENT RAYMOND, O. M. C., J. C. D., The Approbation of Religious Institutes, 171 pp., 1931.
72. PERNICONE, REV. JOSEPH M., A. B., J. C. D., The Ecclesiastical Prohibition of Books, XII-267 pp., 1932.
73. CLINTON, REV. CONNELL, A. B., J. C. D., The Paschal Precept, IX-108 pp., 1932.
74. DONNELLY, REV. FRANCIS B., A. M., S. T. L., J. C. D., The Diocesan Synod, VIII-125 pp., 1932.
75. TORRENTE, REV. CAMILO, C. M. F., J. C. D., Las Procesiones Sagradas, V-145 pp., 1932.
76. MURPHY, REV. EDWIN J., C. PP. S., J. C. D., Suspension Ex Informata Conscientia, XI-122 pp., 1932.
77. MACKENZIE, REV. ERIC F., A. M., S. T. L., J. C. D., The Delict of Heresy in its Commission, Penalization, Absolution, VII-124 pp., 1932.
78. LYONS, REV. AVITUS E., S. T. B., J. C. D., The Collegiate Tribunal of First Instance, XI-147 pp., 1932.
79. CONNOLLY, REV. THOMAS A., J. C. D., Appeals, XI-195 pp., 1932.
80. SANGMEISTER, REV. JOSEPH V., A. B., J. C. D., Force and Fear as Precluding Matrimonial Consent, V-211 pp., 1932.
81. JAEGER, REV. LEO A., A. B., J. C. D., The Administration of Vacant and Quasi-Vacant Episcopal Sees in the United States, IX-229 pp., 1932.
82. RIMLINGER, REV. HERBERT T., J. C. D., Error Invalidating Matrimonial Consent, VII-79 pp., 1932.
83. BARRETT, REV. JOHN D. M., S. S., J. C. D., A Comparative Study of the Councils of Baltimore and the Code of Canon Law, IX-223 pp., 1932.

84. Carberry, Rev. John J., Ph. D., S. T. D., J. C. D., The Juridical Form of Marriage, X-177 pp., 1934.
85. Dolan, Rev. John L., A. B., J. C. D., The Defensor Vinculi, XII-157 pp., 1934.
86. Hannan, Rev. Jerome D., A. M., S. T. D., LL. B., J. C. D., The Canon Law of Wills, IX-517 pp., 1934.
87. Lemieux, Rev. Delise A., A. M., J. C. D., The Sentence in Ecclesiastical Procedure, IX-131 pp., 1934.
88. O'Rourke, Rev. James J., A. B., J. C. D., Parish Registers, VII-109 pp., 1934.
89. Timlin, Rev. Bartholomew, O. F. M., A. M., J. C. D., Conditional Matrimonial Consent, X-381 pp., 1934.
90. Wahl, Rev. Francis X., A. B., J. C. D., The Matrimonial Impediments of Consanguinity and Affinity, VI-125 pp., 1934.
91. White, Rev. Robert J., A. B., LL. B., S. T. B., J. C. D., Canonical Ante-Nuptial Promises and the Civil Law, VI-152 pp., 1934.
92. Herrera, Rev. Antonio Parra, O. C. D., J. C. D., Legislación Eclesiástica sobra el Ayuno y la Abstinencia, XI-191 pp., 1935.
93. Kennedy, Rev. Edwin J., J. C. D., The Special Matrimonial Process in Cases of Evident Nullity, X-165 pp., 1935.
94. Manning, Rev. John J., A. B., J. C. D., Presumption of Law in Matrimonial Procedure, XI-111 pp., 1935.
95. Moeder, Rev. John M., J. C. D., The Proper Bishop for Ordination and Dimissorial Letters, VII-135 pp., 1935.
96. O'Mara, Rev. William A., A. B., J. C. D., Canonical Causes for Matrimonial Dispensations, IX-155 pp., 1935.
97. Reilly, Rev. Peter, J. C. D., Residence of Pastors, IX-81 pp., 1935.
98. Smith, Rev. Mariner T., O. P., S. T. Lr., J. C. D., The Penal Law for Religious, VIII-169 pp., 1935.
99. Whalen, Rev. Donald W., A. M., J. C. D., The Value of Testimonial Evidence in Matrimonial Procedure, XIII-297 pp., 1935.
100. Cleary, Rev. Joseph F., J. C. D., Canonical Limitations on the Alienation of Church Property, VIII-141 pp., 1936.
101. Glynn, Rev. John C., J. C. D., The Promoter of Justice, XX-337 pp., 1936.
102. Brennan, Rev. James H., S. S., M. A., S. T. B., J. C. D., The Simple Convalidation of Marriage, VI-135 pp., 1937.
103. Brunini, Rev. Joseph Bernard, J. C. D., The Clerical Obligations of Canons 139 and 142, X-121 pp., 1937.
104. Connor, Rev. Maurice, A. B., J. C. D., The Administrative Removal of Pastors, VIII-159 pp., 1937.
105. Guilfoyle, Rev. Merlin Joseph, J. C. D., Custom, XI-144 pp., 1937.
106. Hughes, Rev. James Austin, A. B., A. M., J. C. D., Witnesses in Criminal Trials of Clerics, IX-140 pp., 1937.

107. JANSEN, REV. RAYMOND J., A. B., S. T. L., J. C. D., Canonical Provisions for Catechetical Instruction, VII-153 pp., 1937.
108. KEALY, REV. JOHN JAMES, A. B., J. C. D., The Introductory Libellus in Church Court Procedure, XI-121 pp., 1937.
109. MCMANUS, REV. JAMES EDWARD, C. SS. R., J. C. D., The Administration of Temporal Goods in Religious Institutes, XVI-196 pp., 1937.
110. MORIARTY, REV. EUGENE JAMES, J. C. D., Oaths in Ecclesiastical Courts, X-115 pp., 1937.
111. RAINER, REV. ELIGIUS GEORGE, C. SS. R., J. C. D., Suspension of Clerics, XVII-249 pp., 1937.
112. REILLY, REV. THOMAS F., C. SS. R., J. C. D., Visitation of Religious, VI-195 pp., 1938.
113. MORIARTY, REV. FRANCIS E., C. SS. R., J. C. D., The Extraordinary Absolution from Censures, XV-334 pp., 1938.
114. CONNOLLY, REV. NICHOLAS P., J. C. D., The Canonical Erection of Parishes, X-132 pp., 1938.
115. DONOVAN, REV. JAMES JOSEPH, J. C. D., The Pastor's Obligation in Prenuptial Investigation, XII-322 pp., 1938.
116. HARRIGAN, REV. ROBERT J., M. A., S. T. B., J. C. D., The Radical Sanation of Invalid Marriages, VIII-208 pp., 1938.
117. BOFFA, REV. CONRAD HUMBERT, J. C. D., Canonical Provisions for Catholic Schools, VII-211 pp., 1939.
118. PARSONS, REV. ANSCAR JOHN, O. M. CAP., J. C. D., Canonical Elections, XII-236 pp., 1939.
119. REILLY, REV. EDWARD MICHAEL, A. B., J. C. D., The General Norms of Dispensation, XII-156 pp., 1939.
120. RYAN, REV. GERALD ALOYSIUS, A. B., J. C. D., Principles of Episcopal Jurisdiction, XII-172 pp., 1939.
121. BURTON, REV. FRANCIS JAMES, C. S. C., A. B., J. C. D., A Commentary on Canon 1125, X-222 pp., 1940.
122. MIASKIEWICZ, REV. FRANCIS SIGISMUND, J. C. D., Supplied Jurisdiction According to Canon 209, XII-340 pp., 1940.
123. RICE, REV. PATRICK WILLIAM, A. B., J. C. D., Proof of Death in Prenuptial Investigation, VIII-156 pp., 1940.
124. ANGLIN, REV. THOMAS FRANCIS, M. S., J. C. D., The Eucharistic Fast, VIII-183 pp., 1941.
125. COLEMAN, REV. JOHN JEROME, J. C. D., The Minister of Confirmation, VI-153 pp., 1941.
126. DOWNS, REV. JOHN EMMANUEL, A. B., J. C. D., The Concept of Clerical Immunity, XI-163 pp., 1941.
127. ESSWEIN, REV. ANTHONY ALBERT, J. C. D., Extrajudicial Penal Powers of Ecclesiastical Superiors, X-144 pp., 1941.

128. Farrell, Rev. Benjamin Francis, M. A., S. T. L., J. C. D., The Rights and Duties of the Local Ordinary Regarding Congregations of Women Religious of Pontifical Approval, V-195 pp., 1941.
129. Feeney, Rev. Thomas John, A. B., S. T. L., J. C. D., Restitutio in Integrum, VI-169 pp., 1941.
130. Findlay, Rev. Stephen William, O. S. B., A. B., J. C. D., Canonical Norms Governing the Deposition and Degradation of Clerics, XVII-279 pp., 1941.
131. Goodwine, Rev. John, A. B., S. T. L., J. C. D., The Right of the Church to Acquire Property, VIII-119 pp., 1941.
132. Heston, Rev. Edward Louis, C. S. C., Ph. D., S. T. D., J. C. D., The Alienation of Church Property in the United States, XII-222 pp., 1941.
133. Hogan, Rev. James John, A. B., S. T. L., J. C. D., Judicial Advocates and Procurators, XIII-200 pp., 1941.
134. Kealy, Rev. Thomas M., A. B., Litt. B., J. C. D., Dowry of Women Religious, IX-152 pp., 1941.
135. Keene, Rev. Michael James, O. S. B., J. C. D., Religious Ordinaries and Canon 198, V-164 pp., 1941 (Printed 1942).
136. Kerin, Rev. Charles A., S. S., M. A., S. T. B., J. C. D., The Privation of Christian Burial, XVI-279 pp., 1941.
137. Louis, Rev. William Francis, M. A., J. C. D., Diocesan Archives, X-101 pp., 1941.
138. McDevitt, Rev. Gilbert Joseph, A. B., J. C. D., Legitimacy and Legitimation, X-247 pp., 1941.
139. McDonough, Rev. Thomas Joseph, A. B., J. C. D., Apostolic Administrators, X-217 pp., 1941.
140. Meier, Rev. Carl Anthony, A. B., J. C. D., Penal Administrative Procedure Against Negligent Pastors, XI-240 pp., 1941.
141. Schmidt, Rev. John Rogg, A. B., J. C. D., The Principles of Authentic Interpretation in Canon 17 of the Code of Canon Law, XII-331 pp., 1941.
142. Slafkosky, Rev. Andrew Leonard, A. B., J. C. D., The Canonical Episcopal Visitation of the Diocese, X-197 pp., 1941.
143. Swoboda, Rev. Innocent Robert, O. F. M., J. C. D., Ignorance in Relation to the Imputability of Delicts, IX-271 pp., 1941.
144. Dube, Rev. Arthur Joseph, A. B., J. C. D., The General Principles for the Reckoning of Time in Canon Law, VIII-299 pp., 1941.
145. McBride, Rev. James T., A. B., J. C. D., Incardination and Excardination of Seculars, XX-585 pp., 1941.
146. Krol, Rev. John T., J. C. D., The Defendant in Ecclesiastical Trials, XII-207 pp., 1942.
147. Comyns, Rev. Joseph J., C. SS. R., A. B., J. C. D., Papal and Episcopal Administration of Church Property, XIV-155 pp., 1942.
148. Barry, Rev. Garrett Francis, O. M. I., J. C. D., Violation of the Cloister, XII-260 pp., 1942.

149. BOLDUC, REV. GATIEN, C. S. V., A. B., S. T. L., J. C. D., Les Etudes dans les Religious Cléricales, VIII-155 pp., 1942.
150. BOYLE, REV. DAVID JOHN, M. A., J. C. D., The Juridic Effects of Moral Certitude on Pre-Nuptial Guarantees, XII-188 pp., 1942.
151. CANAVAN, REV. WALTER JOSEPH, M. A., LITT. D., J. C. D., The Profession of Faith,.XII-143 pp., 1942.
152. DESROCHERS, REV. BRUNO, A. B., PH. L., S. T. B., J. C. D., Le Premier Concile Plénier de Québec et le Code de Droit Canonique, XIV-186 pp., 1942.
153. DILLON, REV. ROBERT EDWARD, A. B., J. C. D., Common Law Marriage, X-148 pp., 1942.
154. DODWELL, REV. EDWARD JOHN, PH. D., S. T. B., J. C. D., The Time and Place for the Celebration of Marriage, X-156 pp., 1942.
155. DONNELLAN, REV. THOMAS ANDREW, A. B., J. C. D., The Obligation of the Missa pro Populo, VII-131 pp., 1942.
156. ELTZ, REV. LOUIS ANTHONY, A. B., J. C. D., Cooperation in Crime, XII-208 pp., 1942.
157. GASS, REV. SYLVESTER FRANCIS, M. A., J. C. D., Ecclesiastical Pensions, XI-206 pp., 1942.
158. GUINIVEN, REV. JOHN JOSEPH, C. SS. R., J. C. D., The Precept of Hearing Mass, XIV-188 pp., 1942.
159. GULCZYNSKI, REV. JOHN THEOPHILUS, J. C. D., The Desecration and Violation of Churches, X-126 pp., 1942.
160. HAMMILL, REV. JOHN LEO, M. A., J. C. D., The Obligations of the Traveler According to Canon 14, VIII-204 pp., 1942.
161. HAYDT, REV. JOHN JOSEPH, A. B., J. C. D., Reserved Benefices, XI-148 pp., 1942.
162. HUSER, REV. ROGER JOHN, O. F. M., A. B., J. C. D., The Crime of Abortion in Canon Law, XII-187 pp., 1942
163. KEARNEY, REV. FRANCIS PATRICK, A. B., S. T. L., J. C. D., The Principles of Canon 1127, X-162 pp., 1942.
164. LINAHEN, REV. LEO JAMES, S. T. L., J. C. D., De Absolutione Complicis in Peccato Turpi, V-114 pp., 1942.
165. MCCLOSKEY, REV. JOSEPH ALOYSIUS, A. B., J. C. D., The Subject of Ecclesiastical Law According to Canon 12, XVII-246 pp., 1942 (Printed 1943).
166. O'NEILL, REV. FRANCIS JOSEPH, C. SS. R., J. C. D., The Dismissal of Religious in Temporary Vows, VIII-220 pp., 1942.
167. PRINCE, REV. JOHN EDWARD, A. B., S. T. B., J. C. D., The Diocesan Chancellor, X-136 pp., 1942.
168. RIESNER, REV. ALBERT JOSEPH, C. SS. R., J. C. D., Apostates and Fugitives from Religious Institutes, IX-168 pp., 1942.
169. STENGER, REV. JOSEPH BERNARD, J. C. D., The Mortgaging of Church Property, 186 pp., 1942.

170. Waldron, Rev. Joseph Francis, A. B., J. C. D., The Minister of Baptism, XII-197 pp., 1942.
171. Willett, Rev. Robert Albert, J. C. D., The Probative Value of Documents in Ecclesiastical Trials, X-124 pp., 1942.
172. Woebber, Rev. Edward Martin, M. A., J. C. D., The Interpellations, XII-161 pp., 1942.
173. Benko, Rev. Matthew Aloysius, O. S. B., M. A., J. C. D., The Abbot *Nullius*, XVI-148 pp., 1943.
174. Christ, Rev. Joseph James, M. A., S. T. L., J. C. D., Dispensation from Vindicative Penalties, XIV-285 pp., 1943.
175. Clancy, Rev. Patrick M. J., O. P., A. B., S. T. Lr., J. C. D., The Local Religious Superior, X-229 pp., 1943.
176. Clarke, Rev. Thomas James, J. C. D., Parish Societies, XII-147 pp., 1943.
177. Connolly, Rev. John Patrick, S. T. L., J. C. D., Synodal Examiners and Parish Priest Consultors, X-223 pp., 1943.
178. Drumm, Rev. William Martin, A. B., J. C. D., Hospital Chaplains, XII-175 pp., 1943.
179. Flanagan, Rev. Bernard Joseph, A. B., S. T. L., J. C. D., The Canonical Erection of Religious Houses, X-147 pp., 1943.
180. Kelleher, Rev. Stephen Joseph, A. B., S. T. B., J. C. D., Discussions with Non-Catholics: Canonical Legislation, X-93 pp., 1943.
181. Lewis, Rev. Gordian, C. P., J. C. D., Chapters in Religious Institutes, XII-169 pp., 1943.
182. Marx, Rev. Adolph, J. C. D., The Declaration of Nullity of Marriages Contracted Outside the Church, X-151 pp., 1943.
183. Matulenas, Rev. Raymond Anthony, O. S. B., A. B., J. C. D., Communication, a Source of Privileges, XII-225 pp., 1943.
184. O'Leary, Rev. Charles Gerard, C. SS. R., J. C. D., Religious Dismissed After Perpetual Profession, X-213 pp., 1943.
185. Power, Rev. Cornelius Michael, J. C. D., The Blessing of Cemeteries, XII-231 pp., 1943.
186. Shuhler, Rev. Ralph Vincent, O. S. A., J. C. D., Privileges of Religious to Absolve and Dispense, XII-195 pp., 1943.
187. Ziolkowski, Rev. Thaddeus Stanislaus, A. B., J. C. D., The Consecration and Blessing of Churches, XII-151 pp., 1943.
188. Heneghan, Rev. John Joseph, S. T. D., J. C. D., The Marriages of Unworthy Catholics: Canons 1065 and 1066, XVI-213 pp., 1944.
189. Carroll, Rev. Coleman Francis, M. A., S. T. L., J. C. L., Charitable Institutions.
190. Ciesluk, Rev. Joseph Edward, Ph. B., S. T. L., J. C. D., National Parishes in the United States, VI-178 pp., 1944.
191. Coburn, Rev. Vincent Paul, A. B., J. C. D., Marriages of Conscience, XII-172 pp., 1944.

192. CONNORS, REV. CHARLES PAUL, C. S. SP., A. B., J. C. D., Extra-Judicial Procurators in the Code of Canon Law, X-94 pp., 1944.
193. COYLE, REV. PAUL RAYMOND, A. B., J. C. D., Judicial Exceptions, X-142 pp., 1944.
194. FAIR, REV. BARTHOLOMEW FRANCIS, A. B., S. T. L., J. C. D., The Impediment of Abduction, XII-122 pp., 1944.
195. GALLAGHER, REV. THOMAS RAPHAEL, O. P., A. B., S. T. LR., J. C. D., The Examination of the Qualities of the Ordinand, X-166 pp., 1944.
196. GANNON, REV. JOHN MARK, S. T. L., J. C. D., The Interstices Required for the Promotion to Orders, XII-100 pp., 1944.
197. GOLDSMITH, REV. J. WILLIAM, B. C. S., S. T. L., J. C. D., The Competence of Church and State Over Marriages — Disputed Points, X-128 pp., 1944.
198. GOODWINE, REV. JOSEPH GERARD, A. B., S. T. B., J. C. D., The Reception of Converts, XIV-326 pp., 1944.
199. KOWALSKI, REV. ROMUALD EUGENE, O. F. M., A. B., J. C. D., Sustenance of Religious Houses of Regulars, X-174 pp., 1944.
200. MCCOY, REV. ALAN EDWARD, O. F. M., J. C. D., Force and Fear in Relation to Delictual Imputability and Penal Responsibility, XII-160 pp., 1944.
201. MCDEVITT, REV. VINCENT JOHN, PH. B., S. T. L., J. C. L., Perjury.
202. MARTIN, REV. THOMAS OWEN, PH. D., S. T. D., J. C. D., Adverse Possession, Prescription and Limitation of Actions: The Canonical "Praescriptio," XX-208 pp., 1944.
203. MIKLOSOVIC, REV. PAUL JOHN, A. B., J. C. L., Attempted Marriages and Their Consequent Juridic Effects.
204. MUNDY, REV. THOMAS MAURICE, A. B., S. T. L., J. C. D., The Union of Parishes, X-164 pp., 1944.
205. O'DEA, REV. JOHN COYLE, A. B., J. C. D., The Matrimonial Impediment of Nonage, VIII-126 pp., 1944.
206. OLALIA, REV. ALEXANDER AYSON, S. T. L., J. C. D., A Comparative Study of the Christian Constitution of States and the Constitution of the Philippine Commonwealth, XII-136 pp., 1944.
207. POISSON, REV. PIERRE-MARIE, C. S. C., A. B., PH. L., TH. L., J. C. L., Droits Patrimoniaux des Maisons et des Eglises Religieuses.
208. STADALNIKAS, REV. CASIMIR JOSEPH, M. I. C., J. C. D., Reservation of Censures, X-141 pp., 1944.
209. SULLIVAN, REV. EUGENE HENRY, S. T. L., J. C. D., Proof of the Reception of the Sacraments, X-165 pp., 1944.
210. VAUGHAN, REV. WILLIAM EDWARD, J. C. D., Constitutions for Diocesan Courts, X-210 pp., 1944.
211. PARO, REV. GINO, S. T. D., J. C. D., The Right of Papal Legation, X-221 pp., 1944 (Printed 1947).
212. BALZER, REV. RALPH FRANCIS, C. P., J. C. D., The Computation of Time in a Canonical Novitiate, X-227 pp., 1945.

213. DOUGHERTY, REV. JOHN WHELAN, A. B., S. T. L., J. C. D., De Inquisitione Speciali, XII-195 pp., 1945.
214. DZIOB, REV. MICHAEL WALTER, J. C. D., The Sacred Congregation for the Oriental Church, XII-181 pp., 1945.
215. EIDENSCHINK, REV. JOHN ALBERT, O. S. B., B. A., J. C. D., The Election of Bishops in the Letters of Pope Gregory the Great, VIII-200 pp., 1945.
216. GILL, REV. NICHOLAS, C. P., J. C. D., The Spiritual Prefect in Clerical Religious Houses of Study, X-140 pp., 1945.
217. HYNES, REV. HARRY GERARD, S. T. L., J. C. D., The Privileges of Cardinals, XII-183 pp., 1945.
218. MCDEVITT, REV. GERALD VINCENT, S. T. L., J. C. D., The Renunciation of an Ecclesiastical Office, XIV-179 pp., 1945.
219. MANNING, REV. JOSEPH LEROY, J. C. D., The Free Conferral of Offices, VII-116 pp., 1945.
220. MEYER, REV. LOUIS G., O. S. B., A. B., S. T. B., J. C. D., Alms-gathering by Religious, XII-163 pp., 1945.
221. O'DONNELL, REV. CLETUS FRANCIS, M. A., J. C. D., The Marriage of Minors, XII-268 pp., 1945.
222. PRUNSKIS, REV. JOSEPH, J. C. D., Comparative Law, Ecclesiastical and Civil, in Lithuanian Concordat, X-161 pp., 1945.
223. SWEENEY, REV. FRANCIS PATRICK, C. SS. R., J. C. D., The Reduction of Clerics to the Lay State, X-199 pp., 1945.
224. VOGELPOHL, REV. HENRY JOHN, J. C. D., The Simple Impediments to Holy Orders, XVI-190 pp., 1945.
225. BROCKHAUS, REV. THOMAS AQUINAS, O. S. B., J. C. D., Religious Who Are Known as *Conversi*, X-127 pp., 1945.
226. GRIESE, REV. ORVILLE NICHOLAS, S. T. D., J. C. D., The Marriage Contract and the Procreation of Offspring, XVI-224 pp., 1945.
227. BOUDREAUX, REV. WARREN LOUIS, J. C. D., The *"ab acatholicis nati"* of Canon 1099, § 2, XII-110 pp., 1946.
228. BOWE, REV. THOMAS JOSEPH, A. B., J. C. D., Religious Superioresses, VIII-206 pp., 1946.
229. DIEDERICHS, REV. MICHAEL FERDINAND, S. C. J., J. C. D., The Jurisdiction of the Latin Ordinaries over Their Oriental Subjects, XIV-153 pp., 1946.
230. DINGMAN, REV. MAURICE JOHN, A. B., S. T. L., J. C. L., The Plaintiff in Contentious Trials.
231. FRISON, REV. BASIL, C. M. F., M. MUS., J. C. D., The Retroactivity of Law, X-221 pp., 1946.
232. GALVIN, REV. WILLIAM ANTHONY, M. A., J. C. D., The Administrative Transfer of Pastors, XII-288 pp., 1946.
233. GORACY, REV. JOSEPH C., J. C. L., The Diriment Matrimonial Impediment of Major Orders.
234. HALE, REV. JOSEPH FRANCIS, M. A., S. T. L., J. C. D., The Pastor of Burial, X-247 pp., 1946 (Printed 1949).

235. Henry, Rev. Joseph Arthur, A. B., J. C. D., The Mass and Holy Communion: Interritual Law, XII-138 pp., 1946.
236. Linenberger, Rev. Herbert, C. PP. S., J. C. D., The False Denunciation of an Innocent Confessor, VIII-205 pp., 1946 (Printed 1949).
237. Lowry, Rev. James Martin, A. B., J. C. D., Dispensation from Private Vows, XII-266 pp., 1946.
238. Lynch, Rev. George Edward, A. B., S. T. L., J. C. D., Coadjutors and Auxiliaries of Bishops, X-107 pp., 1946 (Printed 1947).
239. Lynch, Rev. Timothy, M. S. SS. T., J. C. D., Contracts between Bishops and Religious Congregations, XIII-232 pp., 1946.
240. McClunn, Rev. Justin David, A. B., S. T. L., J. C. D., Administrative Recourse, VII-142 pp., 1946.
241. Lohmuller, Rev. Martin Nicholas, A. B., J. C. D., The Promulgation of Law, XII-140 pp., 1947.
242. McGrath, Rev. James, A. B., J. C. D., The Privilege of the Canon, XII-156 pp., 1946.
243. Marbach, Rev. Joseph Francis, A. B., J. C. D., Marriage Legislation for the Catholics of the Oriental Rites in the United States and Canada, XIV-314 pp., 1946.
244. Shimkus, Rev. Bernard Aloysius, A. B., J. C. L., The Determination and Transfer of Rite.
245. Smith, Rev. Vincent Michael, A. B., S. T. L., J. C. L., Ignorance Affecting Matrimonial Consent.
246. Wachtrle, Rev. Paul Anthony, A. B., J. C. L., The Baptism of the Children of Non-Catholics.
247. Crotty, Rev. Matthew M., J. C. D., The Recipient of First Holy Communion, X-142 pp., 1947.
248. Eagleton, Rev. George, J. C. D., The Quinquennial Faculties, Formula IV, XIV-199 pp., 1947 (Printed 1948).
249. Gibbons, Rev. Marion L., C. M., LL. B., J. C. D., Domicile of the Wife Unlawfully Separated from Her Husband, XIV-171 pp., 1947.
250. Kelly, Rev. Bernard M., S. T. L., J. C. D., The Functions Reserved to Pastors, IX-141 pp., 1947.
251. Kilcullen, Rev. Thomas J., LL. M., J. C. D., The Collegiate Moral Person as Party Litigant, X-150 pp., 1947.
252. Lafontaine, Rev. Germain J., W. F., J. C. D., Relations Canoniques entre Le Missionnaire et Ses Superieurs, X-117 pp., 1947.
253. Lane, Rev. Loras T., A. B., S. T. L., J. C. D., Matrimonial Procedure in the Ordinary Court of Second Instance, XVI-184 pp., 1947.
254. Lover, Rev. James F., C. SS. R., J. C. D., The Master of Novices, X-168 pp., 1947.
255. McNicholas, Rev. Timothy J., J. C. L., The *Septimae Manus* Witness.
256. Marositz, Rev. Joseph J., M. S. C., J. C. D., Obligations and Privileges of Religious Promoted to the Episcopal or Cardinalitial Dignities, XII-180 pp., 1947.

257. MURPHY, REV. FRANCIS J., A. B., J. C. D., Legislative Powers of the Provincial Council, XII-158 pp., 1947.
258. O'BRIEN, REV. ROMAEUS W., O. CARM., J. C. D., The Provincial Superior in Religious Orders of Men, X-294 pp., 1947.
259. PFALLER, REV. BENEDICT A., O. S. B., J. C. D., The *Ipso Facto* Effected Dismissal of Religious, XII-225 pp., 1947.
260. POPEK, REV. ALPHONSE S., M. A., J. C. D., The Rights and Obligations of Metropolitans, XX-460 pp., 1947.
261. RISTUCCIA, REV. BERNARD J., C. M., J. C. D., Quasi-Religious, XVI-318 pp., 1947 (Printed 1949).
262. SONNTAG, REV. NATHANIEL L., O. F. M. CAP., J. C. D., Censorship of Special Classes of Books, XII-147 pp., 1947.
263. STADLER, REV. JOSEPH N., J. C. D., Frequent Holy Communion, X-158 pp., 1947.
264. SZAL, REV. IGNATIUS J., J. C. D., The Communication of Catholics with Schismatics, XII-217 pp., 1947.
265. WAGNER, REV. URBAN S., O. F. M. CONV., J. C. D., Parochial Substitute Vicars and Supplying Priests, IX-126 pp., 1947.
266. QUINN, REV. JOSEPH, M. A., J. C. D., Documents Required for the Reception of Orders, XII-207 pp., 1948.
267. BENNINGTON, REV. JAMES CLEMENT, A. B., J. C. L., The Recipient of Confirmation.
268. BLAHER, REV. DAMIAN JOSEPH, O. F. M., A. B., J. C. L., The Ordinary Processes in Causes of Beatification and Canonization.
269. CLUNE, REV. ROBERT BELL, B. A., J. C. L., The Judicial Interrogation of the Parties.
270. COURTEMANCHE, REV. BASIL F., B. A., J. C. L., The Total Simulation of Matrimonial Consent.
271. DLOUHY, REV. MAUR JOHN, O. S. B., A. B., J. C. L., The Ordination of Exempt Religious.
272. DONOVAN, REV. JOHN THOMAS, PH. B., S. T. L., J. C. D., The Clerical Obligations of Canons 138 and 140, XII-209 pp., 1948.
273. FREKING, REV. FREDERICK W., A. B., S. T. B., J. C. L., The Canonical Installation of Pastors.
274. FULTON, REV. THOMAS B., J. C. L., Prenuptial Investigation.
275. GODLEY, REV. JAMES P., J. C. L., The Time and the Place for the Celebration of Mass.
276. KANE, REV. THOMAS A., A. B., B. S., J. C. D., The Jurisdiction of the Patriarchs of the Major Sees in Antiquity and in the Middle Ages, XII-111 pp., 1948 (Printed 1949).
277. KENNEDY, REV. ANDREW A., J. C. L., The Annual Pastoral Report to the Local Ordinary.
278. KONRAD, REV. JOSEPH GEORGE, J. C. L., Transfer of Religious.
279. KRESS, REV. ALPHONSE, J. C. L., Contumacy in Ecclesiastical Trials.

280. McCartney, Rev. Marcellus Anthony, O. F. M., M. A., J. C. L., Faculties of Regular Confessors.
281. McCaslin, Rev. Edward Patrick, M. A., S. T. L., J. C. L., The Division of Parishes.
282. McElroy, Rev. Francis J., A. B., J. C. L., The Privileges of Bishops.
283. Quinn, Rev. Stephen, M. S. SS. T., J. C. D., Relation between the Local Ordinary and Religious of Diocesan Approval, XII-153 pp., 1948 (Printed 1949).
284. Schneider, Rev. Edelhard Louis, A. D. S., M. A., J. C. D., The Status of Secularized Ex-Religious Clerics, X-155 pp., 1948.
285. Thompson, Rev. Chester J., A. B., J. C. L., The Simple Removal from Office.
286. O'Brien, Rev. Kenneth R., A. B., J. C. D., The Nature of Support of Diocesan Priests in the United States, XVI-162 pp., 1949.
287. Metz, Rev. John E., S. T. L., J. C. D., The Recording Judge in the Ecclesiastical Collegiate Tribunal, X-130 pp., 1949.
288. Reinhardt, Rev. Marion J., S. T. L., J. C. L., The Rogatory Commission.
289. Ortega-Uhink, Rev. Juan, S. J., J. C. L., De Delicto Sollicitationis.
290. Casey, Rev. James V., J. C. L., A Study of Canon 2222, § 1.
291. Allgeier, Rev. Joseph L., J. C. L., The Canonical Obligation of Preaching in Parish Churches.
292. Cahill, Rev. Daniel R., J. C. L., The Custody of the Holy Eucharist.
293. Carr, Rev. Aidan, O. F. M. Conv., S. T. D., J. C. L., Vocation to the Priesthood: Its Canonical Concept.
294. Knopke, Rev. Roch F., O. F. M., J. C. L., Reverential Fear in Matrimonial Cases in Asiatic Countries: Rota Cases.
295. Lavelle, Rev. Howard D., J. C. L., The Obligation of Holding Sacred Missions in Parishes.
296. Mickells, Rev. Anthony B., J. C. L., The Constitutive Elements of Parishes.
297. Noone, Rev. John J., J. C. L., Nullity in Judicial Acts.
298. Sheehan, Rev. Daniel E., J. C. L., The Minister of Holy Communion.
299. Statkus, Rev. Francis J., J. C. L., The Minister of the Last Sacraments.
300. Cook, Rev. John P., J. C. L., Ecclesiastical Communities and Their Ability to Induce Legal Customs.
301. Fazzalaro, Rev. Francis J., J. C. L., The Place for the Hearing of Confessions.
302. Hannan, Rev. Philip M., J. C. L., The Canonical Concept of *congrua sustentatio* for the Secular Clergy.
303. Quinn, Rev. Hugh G., S. T. L., J. C. L., The Particular Penal Precept.
304. Gallagher, Rev. John F., J. C. L., The Matrimonial Impediment of Public Propriety.
305. Welsh, Rev. Thomas J., J. C. L., The Use of the Portable Altar.

www.ingramcontent.com/pod-product-compliance
Lightning Source LLC
LaVergne TN
LVHW050224080826
844660LV00012B/461

* 9 7 8 0 8 1 3 2 2 4 7 6 3 *